A Christian Counselor's Primer On...

For helping those who struggle with.....

Depression

A series of Resource Manuals for Counselors, Pastors, Teachers, Altar Workers, & all those who serve to comfort and equip the Body of Christ.

Book Three

Written by

Debbye Graafsma, bcpc

Awakened!!
Awakened to Grow
Counsel. Classes. Retreats
awakenedtogrow.com

DISCLAIMER

The lesson materials contained in this primer notebook are provided for informational purposes only. These materials, and any or all accompanying materials published by the author, are not in any way intended to diagnose, treat, or evaluate mental illness; nor are they a substitute for professional counseling and care. Those who suffer from the difficulties covered in "A Christian Counselor's Primer On …" series of booklets should seek additional counsel for their unique situation. Optimally, the materials should be worked through with a trained professional counselor.

The information contained herein is provided for educational purposes only. The user assumes all risks. Debbye Graafsma, Awakened to Grow, and their affiliates deny responsibility for any and all misuses of the information provided.

**Awakened to Grow Ministries
P.O. Box 546
Indian Trail, NC 28079
Website: awakenedtogrow.com**

*A Christian Counselor's Primer on Depression; A series of resources for those who help others... Book 3
(ISBN - 978-0-9852680-8-4)*

©2013 Debbye Graafsma, Awakened to Grow. No portion of this manuscript, nor its accompanying materials may be reproduced or stored by any means or in any format without the written expressed consent of the owners.

A Christian Counselor's Primer on…Depression

Table of Contents

Introduction -- 7

Section One.

    Basic Principles of Growth and Healing-- 9

Section Two.

    Let's Talk About Depression--- 19

Section Three.

    Dealing with Depression-- 29

Section Four.

    Assessment and Discovery Tools-- 43

Section Five.

    The Counselor's Role in the Healing Journey-------------------------------------- 55

    Required Choices to Heal --- 59

Section Six.

    What the Bible teaches about Depression--- 76

Section Seven.

    Scriptural Prayer and Supportive Materials.--------------------------------------- 97

Introduction

Dear Fellow Servant,

If you are reading this, you are either considering purchasing this little hand-book or, have already purchased it... Perhaps you are deliberating how you will incorporate it into your ministry or counseling practice. It is my hope that the information contained here will become a tool, to enable and equip you to more effectively hear and Holy Spirit when it comes to helping others. Not only that; but it is my goal to make your efforts even more fruitful, by providing you with Biblical background and lessons to accompany counseling materials.

Each book in this series: "A Christian Counselor's Primer on...." contains current information relevant to its subject, suggested methods of treatment, as well as a series of charts on its topic that I have developed over the past twenty years in private pastoral counseling practice. Over this period of time, I have found my clients respond more positively when I chart out the truths regarding spiritual and emotional conditions. Doing this allows a person to identify their own experience as it relates to the picture presented to them. We then discuss and learn in conversational one-on-one discipling.

Additionally, I have also developed self-assessments and questionnaires for my clients, in order to aid and speed individual discovery. I have included those assessments and/or questionnaires in these hand-books as they relate to the subjects at hand.

At the end of each hand-book are suggested reading lists for you, the counselor, allowing further study, as well as for the client, allowing personal growth and development.

In Christian circles, it is sometimes too easy to give "pat" answers, or "quick fixes," without seeing actual healing and growth take place in the lives of those we are seeking to serve. Such situations render the client feeling inept, or worse, without enough "faith" to find solution. The fact that you are looking at this booklet exempts you from the circles in which those damaging office visits occur. Thank you for your desire to serve: helping and bringing healing to those who are wounded.

That being said, please allow me take a couple of moments to encourage you.

The ministry of providing a safe place for counsel is a vital one. So much brokenness exists in our society today; so much pain. And yet, only one person out of every four people who are referred to a counseling office will actually make the call and follow-through to keep the appointment. And, of those in that 25 percentile, only around half will actually commit to applying the training they receive in sessions, realizing change and growth. That means that together, as counselors, all of us have about a 13% chance of helping anyone! Believe it or not, that is really good news! After all, just one transformed life can change the world!!

Imagine. What could happen if thirteen out of every one hundred people in your sphere of influence became impassioned and empowered to grow, not only emotionally, but spiritually as well?

Years ago, General Motors' famed inventor and head of research, Charles Kettering, made a very wise declaration in describing how his department approached the concept of designing need-meeting vehicles. He said, "A problem well-defined is half-solved." Not only is this statement true when it comes to designing cars, but it is also true when it comes to the process of learning to choose well in living.

When a client can see the "why" of their struggle in growth and healing, they are more than half-way to discovering the repentant heart and desire to change they need to acquire more healing and therefore, health in their Christian Walk! An encounter with God is then just steps away! Hopefully, using the materials contained here will make than encounter a reality!

In the beginning of each volume, I explain a little about how the Father God's principles of healing work when it comes to emotional healing and spiritual development; with each volume building on the prior volume's teaching. Hopefully, this will help you to discover a sense of empowerment and personal mission. After all, that's why each of us began in this helping ministry......

It is my hope to help you and bless you!

Blessings!

Debbye Graafsma, M.Div., D.Min., bcpc
Awakened to Grow Ministries

Section One
Basic Principles of Growth and Healing
(for Books 1-4; Jesus' parable, "The Sower and the Soil")

There are twelve handbooks in the "A Christian Counselor's Primer on…." series. Each of these "quick-study" texts is designed to provide an overview of the subject presented. In discussing the ministry of helping others, it is important that we handle each subject from a Scriptural viewpoint. For books 1-4, we will consider the first parable Jesus Christ told during His ministry on earth: "The Sower and the Soil" as a springboard for basic understanding.

There is such hope and encouragement to be drawn from this parable. And the fact that it was the first parable Jesus told, also gives us a glimpse of the attitude of Abba Father towards us – even when we are in the worst of conditions.

The idea of healing the hearts of men and women began with Jesus. Continually, throughout His ministry on earth, our God spoke to the very roots and cause of the Pain and dysfunction each of us carry: our baggage, if you will. It is His method to say, "You have heard it said – but *I say to you….*" And then He finishes the statement with something that changes the entire perspective on whatever subject He was speaking.

Jesus came to heal. Jesus came to restore. Jesus came to redeem and rebuild those things lost and broken; those parts of us deemed as beyond repair.

The parable of the Sower is particularly precious in my own life, because the Holy Spirit used it in my own life to challenge my personal depth meter when it comes to emotional and spiritual development.

And let me just say this as we begin: Spiritual development and Emotional maturity cannot be separated. It is impossible to become a healthy, emotionally congruent individual, without finding ourselves at a crossroads of sorts. What will I do with the spiritual issues that stir in my soul when I decide I want to experience "more?" What answers will I allow to pervade and influence my mind and heart? By the same token, personal spiritual development cannot become a reality, unless I choose to yield yet again to the Holy Spirit of the Living God, and allow Him to challenge, confront, and change the attitudes and patterns of my dysfunctional past; allow Him to mold and form on deeper and deeper core levels, His nature and Personality within me….

Jesus Christ was a master Storyteller. In imparting Life-truths, He would weave a story that people related to and were fascinated by. The Sower and the Soil is one of my favorites. Jesus explained this particular parable as being about the human heart; or what we would describe the soul. *(The human soul, is comprised of our mind, will and emotions; what we think, choose and feel.)*

Before we go to the parable, let me share a couple of charts with you, that I hope will serve you well in your desire to help others. When I first began counseling, these were some of the first I developed, and I find I use each of them at least once a day, even now.

The first chart, is the description of the Levels of Relationship and Communication. This is a basic chart that defines the difference between IQ, Intelligence Quotient, and EQ, Emotional Quotient. Emotional Quotient, or Emotional Intelligence, as it is being referred to these days, has to do with one's ability to relate to other people. EQ has to do with the deeper levels of living we all experience with the people we are closest to in relationships.

Jesus referred to the Emotional Quotient, as the "Heart of Man."

Please consider the IQ/EQ chart below.

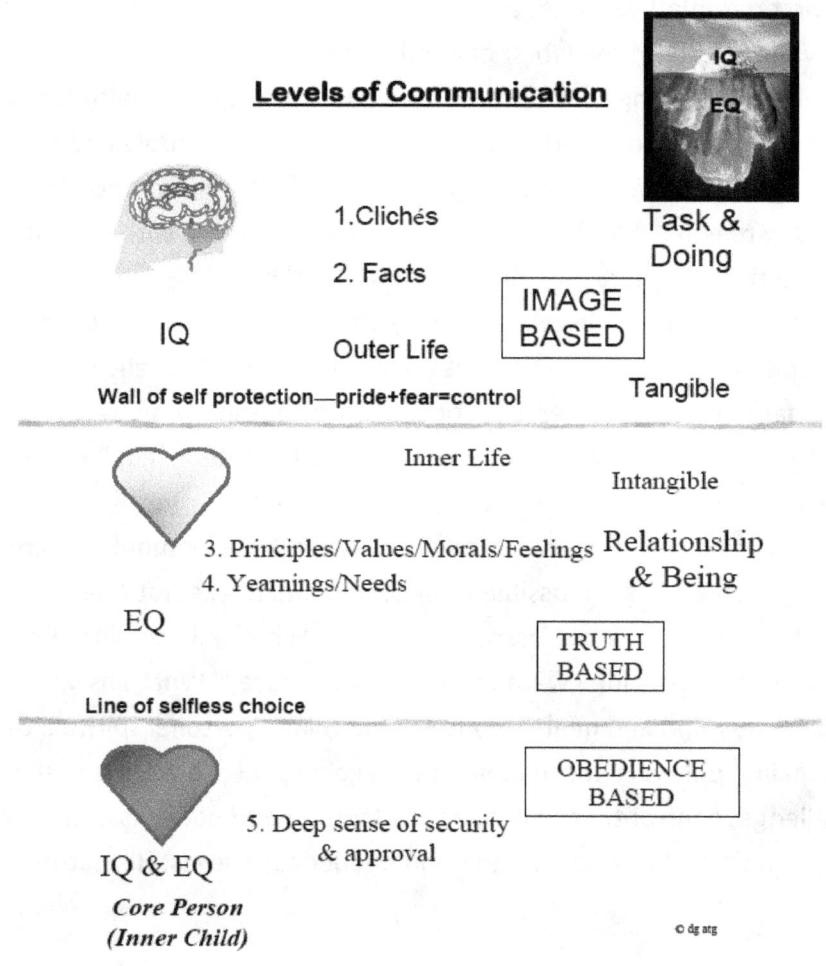

When we study this chart, we discover the differing depths of relationship each of us experience in our lives.

Level 1 = Cliches — These are the people we meet once on an elevator, or in a crowded room, and make **surface-level conversation** with, experiencing no fear or sense of risk.

Level 2= Facts — These are the relationships we encounter in our lives who require **a little more expenditure from us – but still without emotional impartation.** For example, when we are in school, we must memorize and repeat the facts. How well we remember many of the facts determines our Intelligence Quotient. (That is, "are we intelligent, able to apply the facts?" Also, "how well do our life achievements 'stack up' against others' lives, etc.")

A life lived on only levels 1 and 2 will be image based, success oriented, shallow in nature, and dependent upon performance orientation.

Between levels 2 and 3, there exists a Wall of Self-Protection. The wall is comprised of Pride and/or Fear. Simply put, Fear + Pride = Control. Most of us construct our personal wall in pre-puberty, or just after, depending upon the comparisons we make between our "nest" and the "nests" of those in our friendship circle, and how our own sense of "normal" compares to the "normal" of our friends and acquaintances.

Level 3 = A ***man*** will experience Level 3 of relationships when he is able to determine his personal **principles and values**, and express them to his companions. A ***woman*** will experience Level 3 in relationships when she is able to express her **morals and feelings** to her companions. There are reasons for these differences in approaching this level of relationship differently; gender being the main reason.

Level 4 = **Yearnings and needs** are what make up the deepest part of our being. In this level, we are able to share our hopes and dreams as they relate to our future. These are the deepest perceived needs we carry; many times without expression.

A life lived incorporating levels 3 and 4 into daily experience, will manifest the Personhood of a well-bonded individual. Such a person has chosen to cease trying to "hold to the image" of who he or she believes must be portrayed in day to day living.

However, what actually fuels, or gives power to, the Emotional Quotient levels of our lives is the substance of Truth. In places where we have learned to believe our experiences as being the source of Truth, we will develop broken trust and an inability to relate to others in a healthy way. (This is something we all do.)

When we become believers in Christ, the Holy Spirit begins the process of personal transformation; bringing comfort, healing, change and growth. In the midst of this maturation, there comes a point in the life of every believer when he or she is confronted with the realization of the disparities and contrasts between what our experiences and taught us to be true, and the Truth of God's Word.

If a person chooses to cling to the perceptions he or she has always believed; the person's own conclusions of "truth;" then the processes of emotional development and spiritual maturation cease. Sadly, when this type of refusal to the Spirit's formation occurs, any future discoveries the believer receives will be tainted by that refusal; influenced by elements of fear and legalism.

In contrast, when a believer is willing to take the risk of trusting God for their emotional development, the Holy Spirit (the Helper and Teacher) continues the process of healthy emotional and spiritual development by breathing courage into the soul. He then will confront the believer with the need to exchange those inward perceptions of "truth" for Abba Father's Truth. When our "truth," or perception, is traded for God the Father's Truth, the Bible becomes a template learning how to live the life of a believer. At that point of growth, the Word of God becomes real to us; more than mental assent.

At that point, *His Truth* becomes voluntarily traded for *our truth*. *His Truth* is durable, unshakable, and trustworthy.

Then, as we continue our lives in Jesus Christ, at some future point of our development, we each must come to another place of choosing. This second choice presents us with as question. Will we allow the Holy Spirit to deepen our resolve and obedience with God?

This is the choice to move forward without looking back. It is at this point we discover that we are disciples of Jesus Christ. This second choice, or "wall," if you will, is the fear which confronts us when we seek to give our lives away, or invest our efforts into a cause that will benefit others. When the choice towards discipleship is make, we become willing to offer something of ourselves to God, and to others, simply for the common good. We do it with a sense of purpose and fulfillment, and it is an offering that comes from deep within.

This deepest part of us, I refer to as the Core, or Inner Child.

Now, let's take a look at how those levels of communication affect our personal relationships.

The journey of the Christian life is one that takes us inward, as well as one that focuses our intentions outward. The inward journey of personal Discovery and Empowerment requires the confronting of imprinting, pain and experiences with cause us to be malformed in our emotional growth and development. This is what only the Creator can re-imprint and heal. After all, God is the only Perfect Parent. The outward journey determines the direction of our personal development. It also maintains our balance. In this journey, the Holy Spirit teaches us how to express His care and love for others – without pretense or fear, as disciples of the Living God.

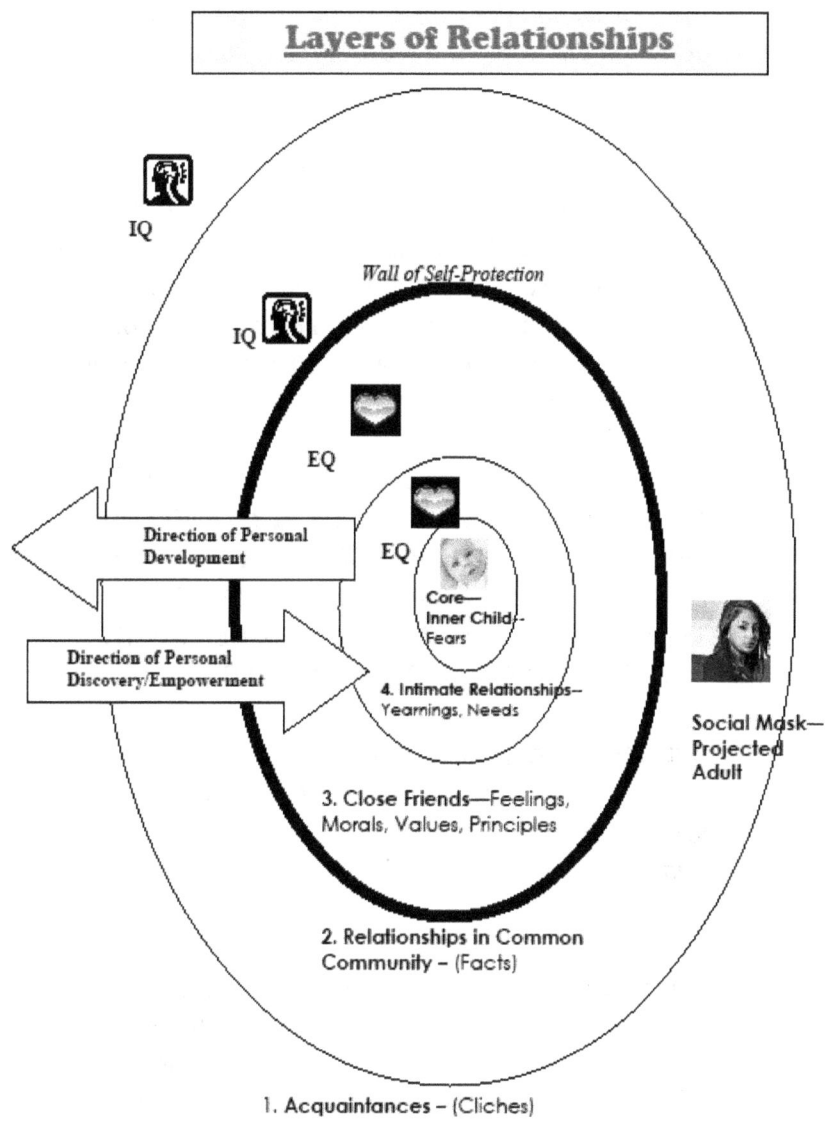

Jesus continually referred to this growth and discovery process. In Matthew 13, our Savior told a parable about a sower, his seed, and the soil.

> *"That day Jesus went out of the house and was sitting by the sea. And large crowds gathered to Him, so He got into a boat and sat down, and the whole crowd was standing on the beach. And He spoke many things to them in parables, saying, "Behold, the sower went out to sow; and as he sowed, some seeds fell beside the road, and the birds came and ate them up. Others fell on the rocky places, where they did not have much soil; and immediately they sprang up, because they had no depth of soil. But when the sun had risen, they were scorched; and because they had no root, they withered away. Others fell among the thorns, and the thorns came up and choked them out. And others fell on the good soil and yielded a crop, some a hundredfold, some sixty, and some thirty. He who has ears, let him hear.*
>
> *And the disciples came and said to Him, "Why do You speak to them in parables?" Jesus answered them, "To you it has been granted to know the mysteries of the kingdom of heaven, but to them it has not been granted. For whoever has, to him more shall be given, and he will have an abundance; but whoever does not have, even what he has shall be taken away from him. Therefore I speak to them in parables; because while seeing they do not see, and while hearing they do not hear, nor do they understand.*
>
> *In their case the prophecy of Isaiah is being fulfilled, which says, YOU WILL KEEP ON HEARING, BUT WILL NOT UNDERSTAND; YOU WILL ON SEEING, BUT WILL NOT PERCEIVE; FOR THE HEART OF THIS PEOPLE HAS BECOME DULL, WITH THEIR EARS THEY SCARCELY HEAR, AND THEY HAVE CLOSED THEIR EYES, OTHERWISE THEY WOULD SEE WITH THEIR EYES, HEAR WITH THEIR EARS, AND UNDERSTAND WITH THEIR HEART AND RETURN, AND I WOULD HEAL THEM.'*
>
> *But blessed are your eyes, because they see; and your ears, because they hear. For truly I say to you that many prophets and righteous men desired to see what you see, and did not see it, and to hear what you hear, and did not hear it.*
>
> *Hear then the parable of the sower. When anyone hears the word of the kingdom and does not understand it, the evil one comes and snatches away what has been sown in his heart. This is the one on whom seed was sown beside the road. The one on whom seed was sown on the rocky places, this is the man who hears the word and immediately receives it with joy; yet he has no firm root in himself, but is only temporary, and when affliction or persecution arises because of the word, immediately he falls away. And the*

one on whom seed was sown among the thorns, this is the man who hears the word, and the worry of the world and the deceitfulness of wealth choke the word, and it becomes unfruitful. And the one on whom seed was sown on the good soil, this is the man who hears the word and understands it; who indeed bears fruit and brings forth, some a hundredfold, some sixty, and some thirty."

In this parable, Jesus speaks of four different levels of soil. He likens each level of soil to a condition of a person's soul. As you read, consider and remember the four levels of communication, and the four levels of relationship.

1. Trampled, hardened – describing the soul of a person who does not understand Kingdom life, and who dismisses the Word as not being necessary for living.

2. Rocky, shallow – describing the soul of a person who has many hard and stony places in their heart. They can hear the Truth and have a desire to learn, until they are corrected or confronted. They lack the ability to follow through, and things outside the Presence of God gain attention and loyalty.

3. Weedy, thorny – describing the soul of a person who has battles with distraction in their desire to walk a solid walk with Jesus.

4. Good soil – 30, 60 and 100 fold – describing the soul of a person who receives the seed of God's Truth with an open heart and responds with obedience and teach-ability. Notice that good soil has degrees of fruitfulness.

In this parable, Jesus refers to these differing qualities of soil as being descriptive of the state of the heart of man. This was the first parable Jesus told in His ministry on earth; which makes it highly significant in looking at how God views the condition of our soul when it comes to our ability to relate to Him and to Truth. For me personally, it reminds me that Abba Father made man and woman in His image, placing them in the Garden of Eden to cultivate it and keep it. That would mean that our God has always been a cultivator; a Gardener of the soul, if you will.

What is most encouraging about this parable is that soil quality can be changed. Just like a physical garden, hard work is involved to break up the hard soil, remove the stones, and weeds. And, just like a physical garden, fertilizer is added to soften and enrich the soil. In relational terms, the "fertilizer" which enriches the soil of the heart of man, would be the life lessons (God-given) we take away from the painful experiences in our lives.

As we walk through the first five books in the primer series, please remember the levels of soil, and how they relate to the levels of communication and relationships. Over the past twenty years, I have used these comparisons in the ministry of pastoral counseling; seeing results in the lives of believers as well as disciples.

The four types of soil Jesus referred to in the Sower's parable, directly relate to the four levels of communication and relationship, listed and shown below.

IQ	**1. Cliches**	*Image based – intelligence*
	2. Facts	*Task and Doing oriented*

~~~~~~

EQ	**3. Values, Principles (male)**	*Truth based – heart of man*
	Morals, Feelings (female)	*Relationship and Being oriented*
	4. Yearnings and Needs	

~~~~~~

Core	**Inner Child**	*Real self/spiritual perceptions*
		Obedience and Inner Approval oriented

There are many areas of relational living which correspond to these four levels of relationship. For a more detailed addressing of this subject, and to pinpoint a person's placement in growth, please consider utilizing the G.E.M.S. Personal Assessment Tool, (Section M), by Debbye Graafsma. *(Available through Awakened to Grow, or online.)*

When a person lives in a healthy state, individual Personhood is expressed through the whole being. This is called Congruency. On a practical level, the person portrays the same personality in all settings of living. They are strong enough in their Core to withstand the pressures and intimidations of varying environments.

When we come to Christ, becoming believers for the first time, very rarely is anyone congruent. That process begins when we choose to yield to the Spirit of God, allowing Him access and permission to shape us into the likeness of Christ.

In considering these truths, I have provided a chart on the next page, which combines the work of cultivation or gardening, with the condition of the soil on each level. It is my hope it will encourage you as you encounter believers as well as disciples in your ministry as a helper/counselor.

The Sower and the Seed: Becoming A Cultivated & Well Watered Garden

"The Lord will guide you continually, and satisfy your soul in drought, and strengthen your bones; and you shall be like a watered garden, and like a spring of water, whose waters do not fail." Isaiah 58:11

The Parable: Matthew 13:3-9 and 18-23

Type of Soil Vs 3-9	Jesus' Meaning vs 18-23	Condition of the Heart	A Gardener's Solution	Spiritual Application
1. Seed on the wayside -- was devoured by birds	Not understood. Devil steals it. Survivor mentality	Numb, Trodden down. By reason of conditioning has become rock hard feels used.	Soak with water. Break up crusty earth. Dig deep earth. Dig. Remove rocks. Add fertilizer and conditioners before planting. Feed well.	Has learned to believe a lie. Life experiences have wounded and closed the heart. (emotionally and spiritually)
2. Seed on stony places -- no depth, withered by elements	Receives, but has No depth in himself to make application, is offended by difficulty and falls away only. No joy. "Tell me what the rules are – I'll do that."	Unaware of deeper possibilities. Too many hard things with no understanding or ability to resolve. Functioning plants well.	Water well to loosen earth. Remove stones. Dig down to rock. Add fertilizer and conditioners. Feed	Sees the stones. Feel stuck. Difficulties argue with the love of God. The heart wants to trust, but fears repetition of pain. (trusts self most)
3. Seed among thorns -- new growth crowded by weeds	Receives, but has so many other things "going on right now" any application is squeezed out, becomes unfruitful	Aware of deeper growth. Drawn by Holy Spirit -- is easily distracted by obligations and responsibilities. Content to maintain on surface but lives unfulfilled	Weed out crowded growth beds. Spade around plants for aerating soil. Add fertilizer. Condition soil. Water well. Monitor for sprouts of weed seeds not pulled on first try.	Is weed aware, assumes they are normal – is used to emotional clutter. Fearful of Change – task oriented for security. (works based. Condemnation focused, fear driven)
4. Seed on good ground -- yielded a crop	Receives, understands, allows it to grow, and bears life-fruit	Open and vulnerable. Teachable, receiving truth and making application personal changes daily indicate growth	Maintain weed free status. Maintain condition of soil. Regular cultivation and aeration for health. New plantings and pruning as applicable.	Maturity takes time, growth takes time. There are no substitutes. Discipleship involves discovery. Emotional health and spiritual maturity cannot be separated. Daily maintenance will ensure continued development.

Section Two
Let's Talk About Depression

"What is Depression? How Do I Recognize it?"

What is it about the word "depression" that sparks a negative reaction in most Christians? Is it somehow a weakness, or a sign of a lack of faith? Is it possible to be a committed and growing disciple of Jesus Christ and struggle with issues of discouragement, or depression?

After all, shouldn't a "strong" Christian be able to "just get over it?"

Depression has many forms. More than 65% of all Americans will deal with a major form of depression in their lifetime. Those who suffer from what has been called the "common cold of the soul," are also found within the church walls. It is important as Christian counselors, we provide a kind, gentle, and safe environment in which a person may unload their pain, and then gradually come to discovery of its causes.

This year in the United States:
- 19 million adults will suffer from a major form of depression
- 10-15% of all children and teens will experience depression at any given time
- More than 1 million teens, age 14 or older will experience a major bout with depression
- 70-80% of American adults will be affected by depression in one way or another
- 2% of children under twelve will experience depression
- Untreated depression (4months or longer in duration) will end in suicide.

Depression can show itself in several different forms. It can manifest in anxiety, panic attacks, and struggles with Fear. Usually, a bout with Depression can last for several months in an adult, most often in response to an unprocessed Grief, Loss, or Life-Change. A slighter exhibition of Depression, known as Dysthymia, is much harder to recognize, even though it lasts much longer than several months. Dysthymia can last as long as seven or eight years, and can many times be remembered by depressed adults as the beginning of their long-term problems.

When children suffer from depression, dysthymia, or even anxiety, the symptoms will show themselves in physical complaints, known as "somatic." In a non-depressed child, these somatic complaints might manifest for a few weeks at a time, due to a specific cause. However, in a depressed child, the longevity of the symptoms will be months or even years. These symptoms are:

    Emotional withdrawal
    Clingy behavior
    Separation anxiety
    Chronic boredom
    Anti-social behaviors
    Anger

Surprisingly, during elementary years (ages 3-12), boys have a higher rate of depression than their counterparts. It is easy to miss depression in a young boy, due to the high percentage of acting out in young males. As adolescence approaches, girls will begin to manifest the same percentages of experiencing depression as adult women; which is twice or three times the occurrence as the male population.

Most of the time, depression in children finds its catalyst in one or all of the following categories:

    A depressed mother (the child has absorbed the mother's emotion)
    No teaching of social/people skills or manners
    The absorption of negative environment factors (rejection, anger, criticism, abuse)
    Divorcing parents
    Fighting parents
    Pessimism

Adults with the same struggle with Depression might manifest any or all of the following symptoms:

    Sad, disheartened mood; outbursts of anger
    Withdrawal from friends or social situations
    Loss of interest in activities normally enjoyed
    Loss of appetite or overeating; other addictions/substance abuse
    Inability to make a decision
    Loss of energy
    Feeling hopeless; worthlessness
    Headaches
    Loss of self-esteem; feeling an overall sense of guilt
    Difficulty concentrating
    Neck/Shoulder Pain; Joint or lower back pain
    Suicidal thoughts or Attempts of suicide

Depression is one of the primary causes of heart disease, and is a seedbed for many stress based diseases.

Depression erupts from the deepest parts of our Personhood. It draws its fuel from our painful experiences, and seeks to isolate us from connecting with the healing and growth we each so desperately need. When we have gained the emotional tooling to work through a depressing situation, we are able to process it more quickly. When those tools are missing in our emotional "tool-kit," we might try the wrong tools (such as rage, control, etc.), to help ourselves survive.

That being said, it is important to remember that most people who deal with Depression are actually in the midst of a grieving process. Usually, clients show up in my own office because they feel "stuck" and are unable to move forward with their lives. We then do a little investigative work to discover what losses they might possibly be in the midst of grieving; and then, what concerns or fears are hindering their growth progression.

The deepest parts of our soul are levels 3, 4 and 5 in the levels of Communication and Relationship. These are areas of living which develop during our early years. We must be taught to communicate and relate regarding our feelings, our values, our yearnings and needs; regarding our core perceptions. Communication and vulnerability are learned skills, designed by God to be established in a safe community, where mistakes are accepted as expected elements in the learning process.

It has been my experience in counseling, as well as during my own bouts with Depression, that the "dark cloud" must be dealt with, or it will compound into a thunderstorm in the soul when the next crisis occurs. When I say "dealt with," I mean processed for growth and healing.

There are no time limits to Depression. While one widow might grieve her husband for one year and be able to move forward, another might begin a cycle of repetitive emotions and behaviors and grieve for many years. The difference between the two experiences is, in my experience, the amount of emotional tooling and safe community the client receives in their life environment.

On the following pages are several basic charts on emotional development which I developed for use when a client presents with a problem like Depression. These, along with Personality evaluations, some behavioral analysis, and probable usage of one or more of the self-assessments contained in this handbook, help to stimulate the client to communicate.

Providing a gentle and accepting environment is a key for a client dealing with Depression. The most important step is the first step – Once a client can unload what they feel to someone who is invested enough to really listen, the process begins.

From that point onward, my personal goal is always to lead the client to discovery, and then a realization of purpose in recovering.

Did you know?

Many Biblical "heroes" dealt with forms of Depression. So those who face what they feel are in company with the most courageous of truly spiritual people....

Just look at the list:

Job, Jeremiah, King Hezekiah, Elijah, King David, Saul, Peter, Esther, Naomi, Joseph..... and even Jesus in Gethsemane....

Each of these individuals dealt with forms of depression. So why would anyone choose to believe God is not near to us when we are experiencing seasons of Depression?

In fact, it is in the "dark seasons," when our Shepherd and Great Physician will meet us; intersecting His life with our own

– to Comfort, Heal and Restore.

It is always helpful for a client to discover how deeply they are in touch with their emotional life. Do they feel deeply? Are they walled off? Do they avoid relationships requiring vulnerability? Are they confident to allow themselves to be known, and to relate to others?

Levels of Communication

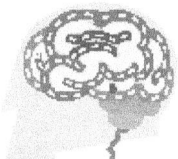

1. Clichés
2. Facts

IQ

Outer Life

Task & Doing

IMAGE BASED

Tangible

Wall of self protection—pride+fear=control

Inner Life

Intangible

3. Principles/Values/Morals/Feelings
4. Yearnings/Needs

Relationship & Being

EQ

TRUTH BASED

Line of selfless choice

OBEDIENCE BASED

5. Deep sense of security & approval

IQ & EQ

Core Person
(Inner Child)

© dg atg

> "O taste and see that the LORD is good;
> How blessed is the man who takes refuge in Him!"
> Psalm 34:8

The Scriptures consistently indicate that relationship with God is designed to be experienced. Rather than remaining on a surface level, the Holy Spirit continually draws each of us to trust Him with our fears, and areas of disappointment. Depression, by its very nature, seeks to defeat and derail the believer's ability to expect God to be good in nature, kind in heart, or even gracious in responses.

> *"Depression is the middle ground between the preserved energy to change, and the total abandonment of hope."* Dr. Dan Allender

Depression can sabotage a person's closest of relationships. Because its source is the deepest parts of the soul, the problem many times resides in a client's inability to communicate their deepest feelings with those who are closest to them. Looking at the chart below, each level of relationship corresponds with the varying degrees of emotional intimacy a person will experience in that relationship. Many times, conflicting levels of emotional relationship will short-circuit true intimacy, sparking conflict, misunderstanding, and depression.

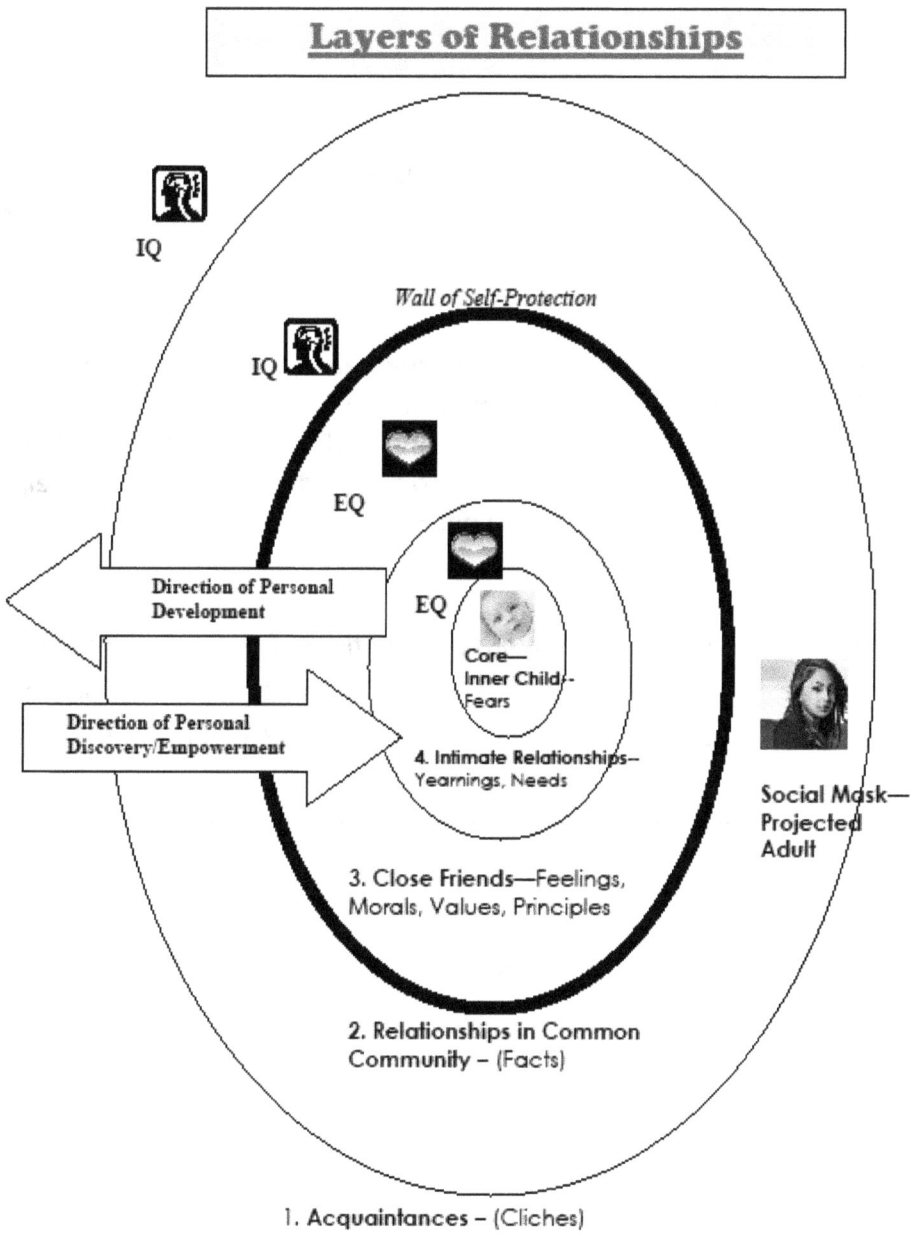

> "Remember the prisoners, as though in prison with them,
> *and* those who are ill-treated, since you yourselves also are in the body."
> **Hebrews 13:3**

One of the main complications Depression causes within a person is an intense focus upon self. Without conscious and intentional choices towards maintaining an objective life-approach, Depression can become all-consuming, and destroy a person's ability to consider the perspectives and feelings of others in regard to day-to-day living. Without help, losing this battle with Depression, can permanently alter a person's ability to relate and/or communicate well.

> *"The way I think determines the emotions I feel. Those emotions will determine the decisions I will make. My decisions predicate my actions, and my actions will define the quality of the life I live."*
> Dr. Chris Thurman

In my own experience, Depression is evidence a person is no longer able to separate deep emotion from non-emotional mental functioning. It is a sign that perceptions learned through negative past experiences, are actually in charge of a person's actions. We are all products of what we have been taught through our past relationships and experiences. Without intentionally addressing our untrue perceptions about how Life is designed to work, we are destined for difficulty and Depression.

Determination Chart

1. Beliefs—

What we believe about how life works as it relates to our own lives, based upon what has shaped us; our experiences, training & modeling.

2. Choices --

Our Perceptions and Evaluations of How Life Works, based on what we have seen work in the past.

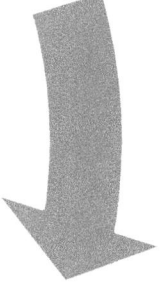

4. Actions –

What we do, moving upon what we assess to be actual and true. These actions reinforce our beliefs, and serve as foundation for greater beliefs.

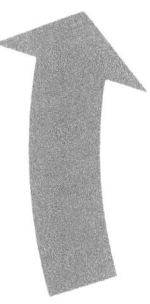

3. Feelings –

What our inner being tells us is true for in regard to life direction; how we must function for survival.

© atg/dcg

Section Three
Dealing with Depression

The Steps of Grief -- *(chart, page 31)*

Over the past thirty years or so, I have had the opportunity to help many people, and see healing come to a spectrum of depression issues. Without exception, in my experience, the problem of depression has manifested during a person's experience with Loss of one form or another. Over the years, the seven Steps of Grief in the chart on the next page have repeated themselves over and over again. Here is an explanation of those steps:

As a catalyst for the grieving process to begin, an incident occurs: whether an abuse, a molestation, a trauma, a death, or an injury of one kind or another. At that point, the steps begin.

Step One.   **Shock.**   *The person feels numb, and is unable to connect with what has happened. They cannot communicate, and many times are in a mental fog. Some traumatic events are blocked out.*

Step Two.   **Denial.**   *The person builds an image of what they wish would happen, or what an acceptable form of Life or a circumstance would look like. I call this a "Denial Bubble." The person then defends and protects that image with one or any combination of defense mechanisms. Defense mechanisms have the ability to distract the emotions, and many times even relationships in the person's life, preventing the admission and processing of what has really happened. In many instances, a person will surround themselves with people who will confirm their denial efforts, even rejecting those who remind them of the Truth of their reality.*

Step Three.   **Hurt.**   *To some extent, whether in surface or in depth, the person begins to move past Denial, into deeper areas of emotional experience. The Reality of the event is admitted (whether partially or completely), and the person begins to sense Hurt and inward Pain.*

Step Four.	**Anger.**	As Pain deepens, the person comes to grips with the injustice of the traumatic event they have suffered. In its pure form, Anger is actually an empowerment to help the person move forward, making positive changes. (For a more complete discussion of Anger, please see "A Christian Counselor's Primer on Anger" (Book 1) by Debbye Graafsma.)
Step Five.	**Depression.**	As Anger fades, or proves to be ineffective in providing the change needed, the person is left with the Truth of their personal Reality. If the person has not dealt properly with their Anger, (allowing Hurt to be disclosed and processed for healing), then the Anger is many times turned inward. This is one form of Depression, however.
Step Six.	**Acceptance.**	When a person begins to move from Depression to Acceptance, they become aware of the differences between their "Denial Bubble," (their former concept of Reality), and their present Reality. The distance in difference between the two extremes will determine the depth of the person's Depression.
Step Seven.	**Resolution & Growth.**	The person does the hard work of bringing together what they thought Life should look like (the "Denial Bubble"), and their present Reality. They make the decision to stop comparing the unattainable with the present, and find themselves able to chart a path to move forward into Health and Healing.

> *"Denial separates the mind from the agony of the heart. A wall of denial is maintained only by the use of costly energies."*
> Wilson

Cycles of Stalled Grief – (chart, page 32)

When a person experiences an inability to walk through all of the Steps of Grief, usually determining that one form or another in the journey is "unacceptable," they will "bounce" off of a step and begin to cycle. The person then continues living in that Cycle of Stalled Grief, until they intentionally address the Pain which caused them to begin the grieving process to begin with. Cycling patterns can be reinforced when additional trauma occurs in a person's life. Unprocessed grief can do a sort of "stockpiling" against the feared (or resisted) step in the Steps of Grief.

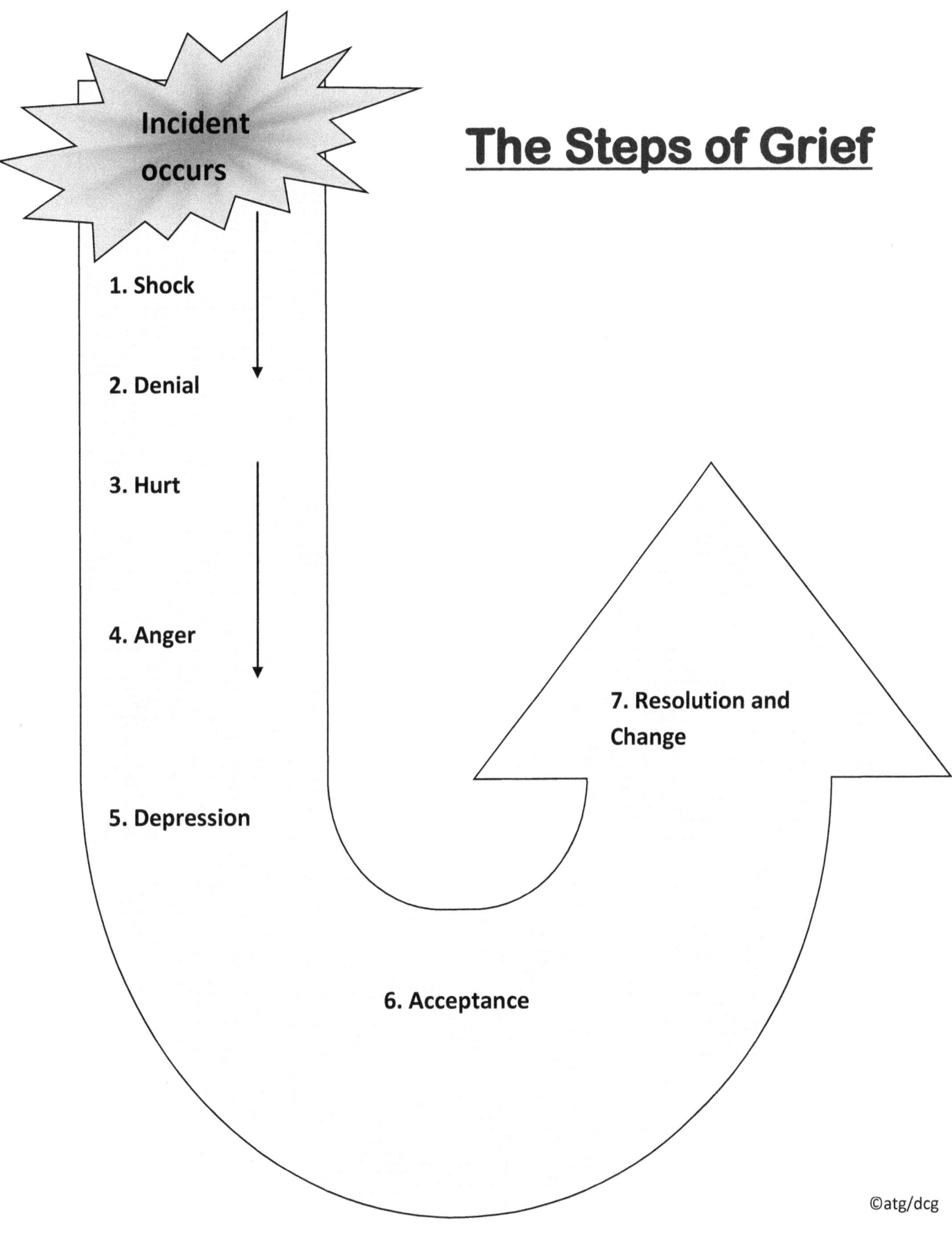

Cyclic pattern Of Stalled Grief

DENIAL'S PING PONG EFFECT

1. blaming
2. placing all fault
3. protesting (justice)
4. control (I'll fix it)
5. bargaining (mental or action)
6. compensating (approval mechanism)
7. minimalizing
8. rationalizing
9. "spiritualizing" – gloss
10. fragmentation
11. withdrawal/retreat
12. addictions
13. coping
14. self-defense
15. legalism/religiosity
16. intense emotional outbursts

denial

hurt

- Takes everything personally
- Sees self as Victimized/defensive
- Centralizes situations back to self
- Low expectations
- Finds it difficult to empathize with others

EVIDENCES OF ANGER

1. Tension/stress release
2. Temper
3. Complaining
4. Bitterness
5. Control
6. Aggression/violence
7. Withdrawal/retreat
8. Non-relational

anger

depression

CAUSES/FORMS OF DEPRESSION

1. clinical depression
2. bi-polar
3. various phobias
4. conduct disorders
5. manic depression
6. schizophrenia

©atg/dcg

Depression has a way of confusing its victim. With Pain clouding a person's ability to reason with clarity, discerning which voice is speaking, a person will many times become afraid to make any decisions or any moves at all towards growth. The chart below has been very effective in helping clients discover the source of their thought patterns.

How to Determine What Is Speaking to You

What God says

When God speaks, the message is accompanied by a sense of approval and affirmation.

We tend to relate to God based on our learning style.

We know we are loved, and personally known.

We feel protected.

He speaks the truth.

He teaches us.

He encourages us.

He gives us understanding.

He gives us direction.

What Self says

When Self speaks, the message is usually focused on our own places of pain. We typically think in "I" statements.

Self says things like:

"I feel _____."

"I wish _____."

What Fear says

When Fear speaks, the message is accompanied by a sense of failure, futility and intimidation. Fear typically speaks in "you" statements.

Fear says things like:

"What if _____."

"You'll never _____."

"What's wrong with you?"

"You should _____."

"You can't _____."

Discovery Keys

1. Stop whatever you are doing. Stand/sit still to think.

2. Focus on what's happening inside you. (think these 3 columns.)

3. Pray in the Spirit. Ask God to help you.

4. Ask Jesus to rescue you and show you what you are hearing.

5. Let your heart relax and receive the love of God for you in that situation.

©2011 dcg/atg

The Survivor vs. Real Self

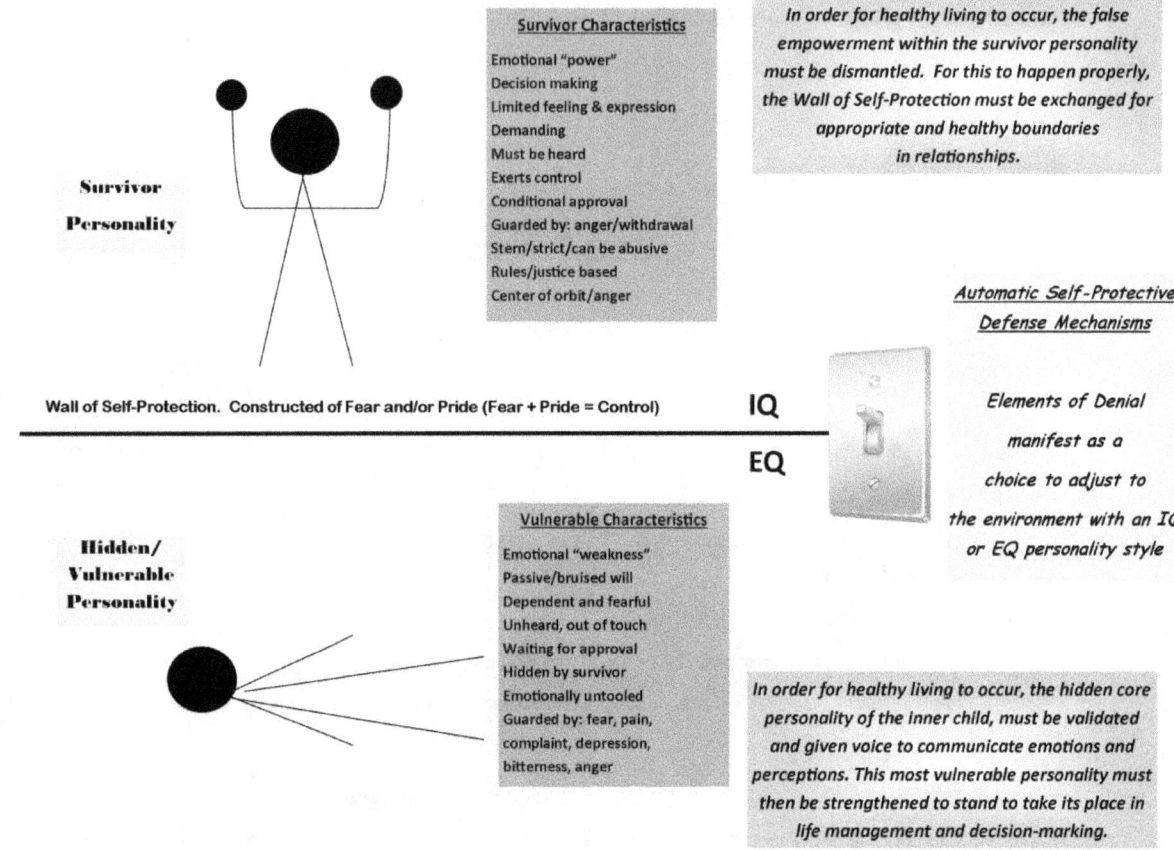

Each of us can recognize within ourselves the quandary described in the chart above. The Survivor Personality is actually an Inner Bully in the experience of most of my clients. It is usually an unwilling copy of faulty adult modeling the person experienced during formative years. The person has learned to reject his or her Real Self, seeking to copy the faulty pattern. Many times, I will ask a client to study the chart and tell me where they might be out of touch with the Hidden/Vulnerable part of their personality. We then discuss the wall of Self-Protection, and how the devices of Denial/Defense Mechanisms actually play into their situation. It can take several sessions for a client to come to discovery. So don't be discouraged or get into a hurry, seeking to make healing happen too quickly. Allow the person to make discovery and encounter Truth.

On the following page, is a charted description of the gears of Self-Hatred. Self-Hatred is the catalyst which fuels the Survivor Self, and teaches the Real Self to allow itself to be shut away.

The Mechanisms of Self-Hatred

The Family life pattern a person has believed to be normal and acceptable also plays into the elements of Depression in the life. Whether known or unknown, a person can sense the absence of healthy bonding during development. This too, can be part of the seedbed for Depression.

Family Diagrams

*Note: Father God's plan and purpose for family life is a safe and secure place; emotionally, physically, and spiritually for each family member. Family Life is a God-created environment where Design and Destiny can be discovered, encouraged, developed and pursued with purpose. While Marriage is a Place **where intimate relationship is developed** between a man and woman who have chosen each other for a life partnership, Family Life is a place **where the children are to be developed** and allowed to grow, encouraged by the parents.*

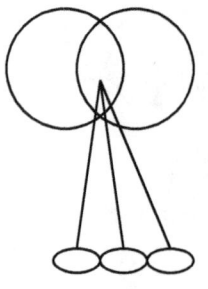

Healthy Family

Father and Mother have learned to operate together, and present decisions and options to children together, as a unified team. Children are ministered to on an equal basis, with no favoritism shown or expressed. **Focus: Abba's plan for the common good.**

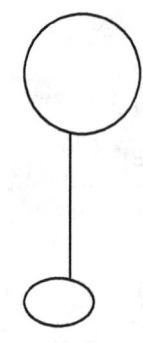

Healthy Single Parent Relationship

Each parent has learned to connect with the child's inner person, and can communicate from a relational point of view future goals and discipline.

Focus: Abba's plan for the common good.

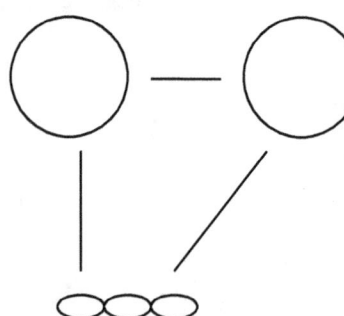

Unhealthy Parent Relationships

Parents are unconnected with each other and with the children. Communication takes place regarding task and fact levels only. Children receive communication, but there is no connection. Result: children receive a sense of abandonment and isolation, and become task oriented for approval. There is little or no affection communicated.
Focus: Personal rights, needs and/or appetites.

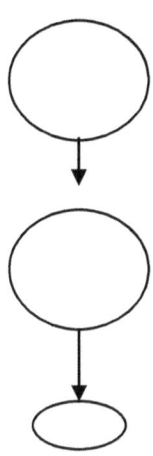

Authority Driven Model (unhealthy)

One parent is seen as having all authority, and communicates with the children through a chain-of-command, without personal relationship with the child. The child is distanced in the relationship and has no opportunity to appeal or question decisions. Voice and Identity are diminished within the family, for all members except the family member with the most authority.

Also within this model, one parent must continually explain the other to the child. The parent in the explaining role tends to lose personal identity and become co-dependent, seeking to keep peace in the home at any price. Acceptance is performance oriented.
Focus: To succeed on all fronts. To meet expectations

The Abuse Model

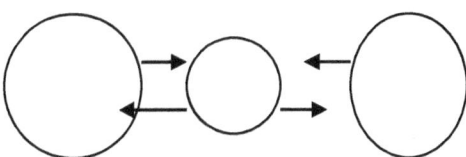

The parents have experienced relational failure in their own abilities to build a marriage. They are emotionally distanced. Communication regarding the relationship is made to the child, and the child feels they must choose between parents.

The child becomes the caretaker, and must meet the emotional needs of the parent; many times this involves verbal, emotional, physical, or sexual abuse (order of progression). The child must continually choose between parents, and perceives they must keep everyone happy. Identity development is stopped, and the child must choose an alternate "power" personality to survive. If a "power" personality is not found, the child will become depressed and lethargic. Approval is shame based
Focus: To survive

The Island Model

The parents have experienced relational failure in their own abilities to build a marriage. They are emotionally distanced. There is no communication.

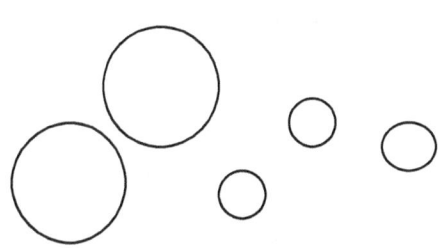

Everyone in the family lives in a separate environment. Everyone Is taking care of themselves, and no one is connected emotionally.

There Is no care on mutual level.
There are no bonding moments that can be remembered in this model
Focus: To survive

The Need for Healthy Attachment/Bonding

When I ask a client to consider the form of their family of origin, I usually ask them to draw their own graph of what family life looked like. From there, it is a short step to ask them to describe the "perfect family," or what they wish their childhood had looked like. In cases where Depression extends to the Core, or Inner Child, this proves to be a wonderful exercise in helping them to embrace the need for change; and their own need to experience healthy attachment and bonding.

That being said; many studies have been done over the past twenty years, regarding the effectiveness of healthy bonding during childhood, and its cause/effect in human development. Without fail, the following were shown to be true regarding the process of Healthy Attachment/Bonding in Human Development:

Most prevalently discovered in the studies I have read over the years, Healthy Bonding provides:

- A sense of confidence
- A personal sense of value
- Stronger communication skills
- Healthy gastric and digestion systems
- More ease in relationships as an adult
- A strong conscience (moral determination of absolutes)
- An ability to label and describe emotions and thoughts
- A desire to help others

Among persons who have had impaired bonding experiences, a uniform detachment is manifested. Detached and unfeeling persons, formerly known as "psycho-pathic" in the counseling field, are now referred to as "socio-pathic" or as exhibiting a "social detachment disorder." These labels communicate the difficulty a person who has no sense of healthy attachment experiences when seeking to live in community, or even family life.

The unconditional Love of God, exhibited in the Body of Christ can become a great source of healing for a person in this state. Indeed, when a person commits to become a disciple of Jesus Christ, the Holy Spirit begins the work of developing what I call "relate-ability" within the life. He guides each of us into all Truth, shaping and forming us into the image of Jesus. He helps us to become "rooted and grounded in love." (Ephesians 3:17)

Levels of Attachment and Conscience Development

Unbonded Unattached	Fragile Or untooled in Bonding	Incomplete Or fractional Bonding	Damaged Or weakened Attachment	Standard or Normal Bonding	Well-Bonded and Attached
Serial Killers Sexual Violence (for pleasure)	Criminals Thieves Prostitutes	Thrill-seekers Some Spies "Danger" addicts	"Charmers," slick presenters, some politicians, "The show must continue mindset"	Intact & well-adjusted families/healthy relaitonships	Humanitarians Those who give their lives for others
Sociopaths Psycopaths (Ted Bundy) (Charles Mansen) (Adolph Hitler)		Narcissists (ego-driven) Prima Donnas			Philanthropists Missionaries (Teresa of Calcutta) (Albert Schweitzer)

FEAR Driven ⟵⟶ **LOVE Led**

Unattached; Unbonded	*Healthy Attachment*
Dulled; Evil Conscience	*Healthy Conscience*
Attachment Disorders	
Impaired Conscience	

FEAR Driven	LOVE Led
Un-motivated	self-disciplines evident
Taker from others — motivated by gain	giving to others
Wrong moral choices — non-contributor	solid moral choices
Critical, laughs at other's pain — passive	sense of humor, laughs at self
Manipulation, "con" — laughs at others	honesty
Rejects relationship — dishonesty, charmer	ability to relate
Feels nothing — hiding in group, loner	ability to feel and process emotion
Stubborn, has no need — feels negative emotion	teachable
Silent, stoic — argumentative, debating	has an ability to communicate
Refuses Truth, alternates own view — responds only	Understands and applies Truth
Negative flow — argues with Truth	creative flow
No hope or future — sporadic flow	half-full perspective
Violence — half-empty perspective	gentleness
Closed, impassive — sarcasm, anger	openness of heart
Bloody images, death — narcissist in heart, abusive	normal fears
— abnormal fears, depressed	

The Substitution Principle

*Somehow, what we **substitute** for the real thing just isn't as fulfilling as the real thing.....*

Emotional Intimacy= The Real Thing

What have we learned to substitute for healthy relationships? How do we cover our Pain? Note: Each of the substitutes listed below have no ability to fulfill in Life to the same degree as actual community care and bonding/attachment. Substitutions fail, and ignite the processes of discouragement and depression.

Which of the following substitutes have you leaned too heavily upon to survive?

1. <u>Money /Success</u> – When a person learns to live in surface areas of IQ only, image becomes extremely important them. The more successful they are, the more achievements they attain, the more money they possess, the more they will become dependent upon those things to determine their value and importance.

   What the Bible says about Money/Success –

   Ecclesiastes 7:12 (NLT)
   "Wisdom and money can get you almost anything, but only wisdom can save your life."

   1 Timothy 6:10 (NKJV) "For the love of money is a root of all kinds of evil. Some people, eager for money, have wandered from the faith and pierced themselves with many griefs."

   Luke 16:13 (NIV) "No one can serve two masters. Either you will hate the one and love the other, or you will be devoted to the one and despise the other. You cannot serve both God and money."

   Matthew 6:19-20 (NIV) "Do not store up for yourselves treasures on earth, where moths and vermin destroy, and where thieves break in and steal. But store up for yourselves treasures in heaven, where moths and vermin do not destroy, and where thieves do not break in and steal.

2. **Conflict Avoidance/Being the "NiceGuy"** – Because a person has been wounded by unhealthy conflict at some point in the past, they might learn to "stuff" their anger, and avoid necessary conflicts. A person might have a misunderstanding of the meaning of boundaries, thinking that establishing a few personal healthy boundaries is wrong behavior, or is selfish. This person then begins to show elements of depression and withdrawal, losing joy in relationships and activities.

   What the Bible says about Conflict Avoidance/Being the "NiceGuy" –

   Matthew 18:15 (NAS) If your brother sins against you, go and show him his fault, just between the two of you. If he listens to you, you have won your brother over.

   Romans 12:18 (NKJV) If it is possible, as much as depends on you, live peaceably with all men.

3. **Expressing Anger/Taking Control –** This person is usually emotionally and relationally un-tooled, and has decided at some point to protect and defend the areas where they are most vulnerable. The problem with choosing this type of substitute is that the person tends to become isolated, and without close relationships.

   What the Bible says about Expressing Anger/Taking Control –

   Romans 16:17 Now I urge you, brethren, note those who cause divisions and offenses, contrary to the doctrine which you learned, and avoid them.

   Psalm 4:4(NKJV) Be angry, and do not sin. Meditate within your heart on your bed, and be still. Selah

   Proverbs 29:22-23 (NKJV) An angry man stirs up strife, And a furious man abounds in transgression. A man's pride will bring him low, but the humble in spirit will retain honor.

   Matthew 5:22 (NKJV) But I say to you that whoever is angry with his brother without a cause shall be in danger of the judgment. And whoever says to his brother, 'Raca!'*(stupid)* shall be in danger of the council. But whoever says, 'You fool!' shall be in danger of hell fire.

   Ephesians 4:25-27 (NKJV) Therefore, putting away lying, *" Let each one of you speak truth with his neighbor,"* for we are members of one another. *"Be angry, and do not sin"*: do not let the sun go down on your wrath, nor give place to the devil.

Proverbs 29:11 A fool vents all his feelings, But a wise *man* holds them back.

Ephesians 4:29-32 Let no corrupt word proceed out of your mouth, but what is good for necessary edification, that it may impart grace to the hearers. And do not grieve the Holy Spirit of God, by whom you were sealed for the day of redemption. Let all bitterness, wrath, anger, clamor, and evil speaking be put away from you, with all malice. And be kind to one another, tenderhearted, forgiving one another, even as God in Christ forgave you.

4. **Trying to be perfect *for* God, *without* God –** This person has many times been involved in a structured form of religious piety, usually without experiencing a deep, inner relationships with God. Perhaps their home environment was controlling, or they are justice centered in their life approach, seeing no need for areas of compromise or compatible relationship development.

    What the Bible says about Trying to be perfect for God, without God –

    Mark 12:29-31 Jesus answered him, "The first of all the commandments *is*: 'Hear, O Israel, the LORD our God, the LORD is one. And you shall love the LORD your God with all your heart, with all your soul, with all your mind, and with all your strength.' This *is* the first commandment. And the second, like *it, is* this: *'You shall love your neighbor as yourself.'* There is no other commandment greater than these."

    Romans 15:13 Now may the God of hope fill you with all joy and peace in believing, that you may abound in hope by the power of the Holy Spirit.

    Isaiah 61:1-3 The Spirit of the Lord GOD *is* upon Me, Because the LORD has anointed Me to preach good tidings to the poor; He has sent Me to heal the brokenhearted, To proclaim liberty to the captives, And the opening of the prison to *those who are* bound; To proclaim the acceptable year of the LORD, And the day of vengeance of our God; To comfort all who mourn, To console those who mourn in Zion, To give them beauty for ashes, The oil of joy for mourning, The garment of praise for the spirit of heaviness; That they may be called trees of righteousness, The planting of the LORD, that He may be glorified."

    Psalm 147:2-4 The LORD builds up Jerusalem; He gathers together the outcasts of Israel. He heals the brokenhearted And binds up their wounds. He counts the number of the stars; He calls them all by name.

Section Four
Assessment and Discovery Tools

On the following pages, are self-assessments for a client
to complete in order to help provide them with
understanding regarding the present influence of Depression in their lives.

Many clients, in making these discoveries,
learn that they are struggling with
Fear, Anxiety, or even Anger. Should this be the case,
assessments from Books 1 and 2 in this series can also be utilized.

How Much Anxiety is Feeding my Sense of Depression?

Based on your present emotions, please assign the number from the statement that most accurately describes how you feel.

1- Always true   2 - Mostly true   3 - Sometimes true
     4 - Hardly ever true   5 - Never true

1. I worry about things that have already taken place.   _____
2. I can become stressed easily.   _____
3. It isn't unusual for me to panic.   _____
4. The things I worry about often turn out to be unimportant.   _____
5. I worry a lot.   _____
6. I tend to feel sad and discouraged more than I would like.   _____
7. I have disturbing thoughts that go through my mind often.   _____
8. I worry often.   _____
9. It isn't unusual for me to lose sleep because I am stressed.   _____
10. I can be easily bothered by circumstances around me.   _____

What is your total score?   _____

Key: **0-11** -- **High levels of anxiety** *(Depression is inevitable)*
             12-24 -- **Considerable levels of anxiety** *(Depression is foreseeable)*
             25-37 -- **Reasonable levels of anxiety** *(Depression is preventable)*
             38-50 – **Low levels of anxiety** *(Depression is remote)*

A person's stage of emotional development is can also be a factor when it comes to dealing with Depression issues. (For a more complete addressing of this issue, please refer to the handbooks in our series entitled, "A Christian Counselor's Primer on Emotional Development," and "A Christian Counselor's Primer on Bonding.") When emotional development is one of the factors in a person's Depression issues, they will many times need to move more slowly through the counseling process.

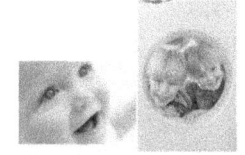
From Child to Adult
Steps to Emotional Maturity

Childhood	Developing Lesson	Adulthood
NO MOTIVATION	Learns to do everything in life for the sake of doing the right thing at the right time — which is Virtue	SENSE OF PURPOSE
REQUIRES INSTRUCTION In order to survive	Discovers that everyone is insecure, and has areas where Life is unknown. Choosing to ask for and seek out help and instruction. This is teachability.	ASKS FOR INSTRUCTION In order to grow
External motivation	Takes responsibility to follow through to completion even those projects and assignments I find unpleasant. Discovers a sense of personal satisfaction in that effort.	Internal motivation
Fear prevents bad behavior	Discovers the depth to which personal negative behaviors affect those in their circles of relationship. Chooses to maintain those relationships rather than satisfy personal urges.	Love/purpose become reasons For healthy Behavior
Shame wants to keep things hidden; maintain image of goodness to gain approval	Realizes that everything happening in our lives is eventually discovered. Choosing to know and be known within safe relationship. Discovering that false images are destructive.	Brings flaws to light in order to heal; honest with self
Avoids getting into trouble; fear of Punishment/disapproval	In light of Christ's love and grace, is willing to own and confess when a mistake is made. Owns responsibility without blame.	Does the right thing, even at personal cost
Avoids discussing unpleasant subjects	Has discovered that everyone on the planet has areas where they are untooled, or uneducated. Has learned the value of non-defensive teachability. Desires to grow.	"Please help me with this"
Seeks to prevent anger from authority figures	Has learned to be open, and known as circumstances happen. Has discovered personal value in relationship with God, so is no longer threatened. Has chosen to value others above self.	Seeks to guard relationship w/ authority figures; accountable
Philippians 3:19 — Driven by flesh God=appetite/Glory= shame	Maturity cannot be rushed. Discovery cannot be forced. Emotional Development takes us from "what's in this for me?" to "what is the right thing for me to do, & when?"	*I Corinthians 13:11— led by love speak, think & reason as an adult*

© atg/dcg

Self Assessment – Am I at Risk for Depression?

1. **Headaches:** Do you suffer from headaches that are not explained by other health conditions?

    _____ Yes   _____ No

    If you answered yes, please rate the intensity and frequency of those headaches

    0   1   2   3   4   5   6   7   8   9   10

    ~~~~

2. **Emotions:** Do you suffer from prolonged sadness? (Two or more weeks at a time)

    _____ Yes   _____ No

    If you answered yes, please rate the intensity and frequency

    0   1   2   3   4   5   6   7   8   9   10

    ~~~~

3. **Emotions:** Do you suffer from a loss of interest in normal activities? (Two or more weeks at a time.)

    _____ Yes   _____ No

    If you answered yes, please rate the intensity and frequency

    0   1   2   3   4   5   6   7   8   9   10

    ~~~~

4. **Emotions:** Do you experience feelings of hopelessness?

   _____ Yes   ____No

   If you answered yes, please rate the intensity and frequency

   0   1   2   3   4   5   6   7   8   9   10

   ~~~~~

5. **Emotions:** Do you find yourself restless or irritable on a regular basis?

   _____ Yes   ____No

   If you answered yes, please rate the intensity and frequency

   0   1   2   3   4   5   6   7   8   9   10

   ~~~~~

6. **Emotions:** Do you have difficulty concentrating?

   _____ Yes   ____No

   If you answered yes, please rate the intensity and frequency

   0   1   2   3   4   5   6   7   8   9   10

   ~~~~~

7. **Emotions:** Do you have difficulty making simple decisions?

   _____ Yes   ____No

   If you answered yes, please rate the intensity and frequency

   0   1   2   3   4   5   6   7   8   9   10

   ~~~~~

8. **Emotions:** Do you have thoughts of death or suicide?

   _____ Yes   ____No

   If you answered yes, please rate the intensity and frequency

   0   1   2   3   4   5   6   7   8   9   10

   If you or someone you know has threatened suicide, you need to speak with someone, or call the national suicide hotline – 1-800-SUICIDE)

   ~~~~

9. **Sleep:** Do you find yourself sleeping too much, or unable to engage in daily life with energy?

   _____ Yes   ____No

   If you answered yes, please rate the intensity and frequency

   0   1   2   3   4   5   6   7   8   9   10

   ~~~~

10. **Sleep:** Do you find yourself having trouble getting to sleep?

    _____ Yes   ____No

    If you answered yes, please rate the intensity and frequency

    0   1   2   3   4   5   6   7   8   9   10

    ~~~~

11. **Sleep:** Do you have other problems that could rob you of your sleep?

    _____ Yes   ____No

    If you answered yes, please rate the intensity and frequency

    0   1   2   3   4   5   6   7   8   9   10

    ~~~~

12. **Sleep:** Do you suffer from prolonged sadness?

_____ Yes   ____ No

If you answered yes, please rate the intensity and frequency

0   1   2   3   4   5   6   7   8   9   10

(Did you know that 80% of people who deal with depression have sleep problems?)

~~~~

13. **Stress and Tension:** Have you experienced a big life event in the past few months?

_____ Yes   ____ No

If you answered yes, please rate the intensity and frequency

0   1   2   3   4   5   6   7   8   9   10

~~~~

14. **Stress and Tension:** Have you experienced two or more life events in the past year?

_____ Yes   ____ No

If you answered yes, please rate the intensity and frequency

0   1   2   3   4   5   6   7   8   9   10

(Sometimes, depression cannot be tied to one event, and it is a response mechanism to a series of events in the life.)

~~~~

15. **Stress and Tension:** Is your life stressful on a day-to-day basis?

_____ Yes   ____No

If you answered yes, please rate the intensity and frequency

0   1   2   3   4   5   6   7   8   9   10

~~~~~

16. **Aches and Pains:** Do you frequently feel pain in the neck, back or shoulders?

_____ Yes   ____No

If you answered yes, please rate the intensity and frequency

0   1   2   3   4   5   6   7   8   9   10

(Joint pain, back pain, headaches, etc, are all common ailments of people who suffer from depression.)

~~~~~

17. **Fatigue:** Do you frequently find yourself without energy, and wonder if it is a lethargy?

_____ Yes   ____No

If you answered yes, please rate the intensity and frequency

0   1   2   3   4   5   6   7   8   9   10

~~~~~

18. **Weight:** Have your gained weight (5 pounds or more) or lost weight (5 pounds or more) in the past month, without trying?

_____ Yes   ____No

If you answered yes, please rate the intensity and frequency

0   1   2   3   4   5   6   7   8   9   10

19. **Stomach-aches and Indigestion:** Do you frequently experience indigestion or gastric pain?

　　　　_____ Yes　　　　____No

　　If you answered yes, please rate the intensity and frequency

　　0　1　2　3　4　5　6　7　8　9　10

　　(45-75% or all depression patients have painful physical symptoms)

~~~~~

20. **Overall sense of life:** Do you feel isolated or disconnected from family and friends?

　　　　_____ Yes　　　　____No

　　If you answered yes, please rate the intensity and frequency

　　0　1　2　3　4　5　6　7　8　9　10

~~~~~

21. **Overall sense of life:** Do you often feel worthless or guilty for no reason?

　　　　_____ Yes　　　　____No

　　If you answered yes, please rate the intensity and frequency

　　0　1　2　3　4　5　6　7　8　9　10

~~~~~

22. **Overall sense of life:** Do you many times feel trapped by a sense of duty?

　　　　_____ Yes　　　　____No

　　If you answered yes, please rate the intensity and frequency

　　0　1　2　3　4　5　6　7　8　9　10

23. **Overall sense of life:** Would you rather withdraw than to engage in large group activities?

    _____ Yes   ____No

    If you answered yes, please rate the intensity and frequency

    0 1 2 3 4 5 6 7 8 9 10

~~~~~

24. **Overall sense of life:** Do you find yourself on the verge of crying often?

    _____ Yes   ____No

    If you answered yes, please rate the intensity and frequency

    0 1 2 3 4 5 6 7 8 9 10

~~~~

25. **Overall sense of life:** Do you find that laughter does not come naturally or easily to you?

    _____ Yes   ____No

    If you answered yes, please rate the intensity and frequency

    0 1 2 3 4 5 6 7 8 9 10

~~~~~

Please go to the next page for scoring,
And information as to what your answers indicate.

Self Assessment – Am I at Risk for Depression?

1. Look back over your answers. How many questions did you answer "yes?"

   _____

2. Please count up the number of questions you answered "yes," and circled a number lower than 4.

   _____

3. How many questions did you answer "yes," and circle a number higher than 4?

   _____

4. Cumulative Scoring: Please add the numbers of the numbers you circled, and assess your risk for depression with the chart below…

50-100 points	**Reasonably Healthy**. Seasonal moods are normal. We all have stressful moments, and times when we wish we were able to accomplish more. Be sure to plan time for soul-care, and for your relationships as you pursue your goals.
100-175 points	**Stressed out**. You are is losing contact with your own personal identity, and should definitely slow down, and reassess your life. Maybe more time for relationship, and less inner pushing. It is time to get rest, and seek help, with choices you are making in making changes.
175-250 points	**Danger zone**. This person is close to a breakdown, and should pursue an immediate lifestyle change, as well as seeking counsel.

Where are you currently living?
Our level of Depression can be determined by our ability or inability to resolve inward conflicts.

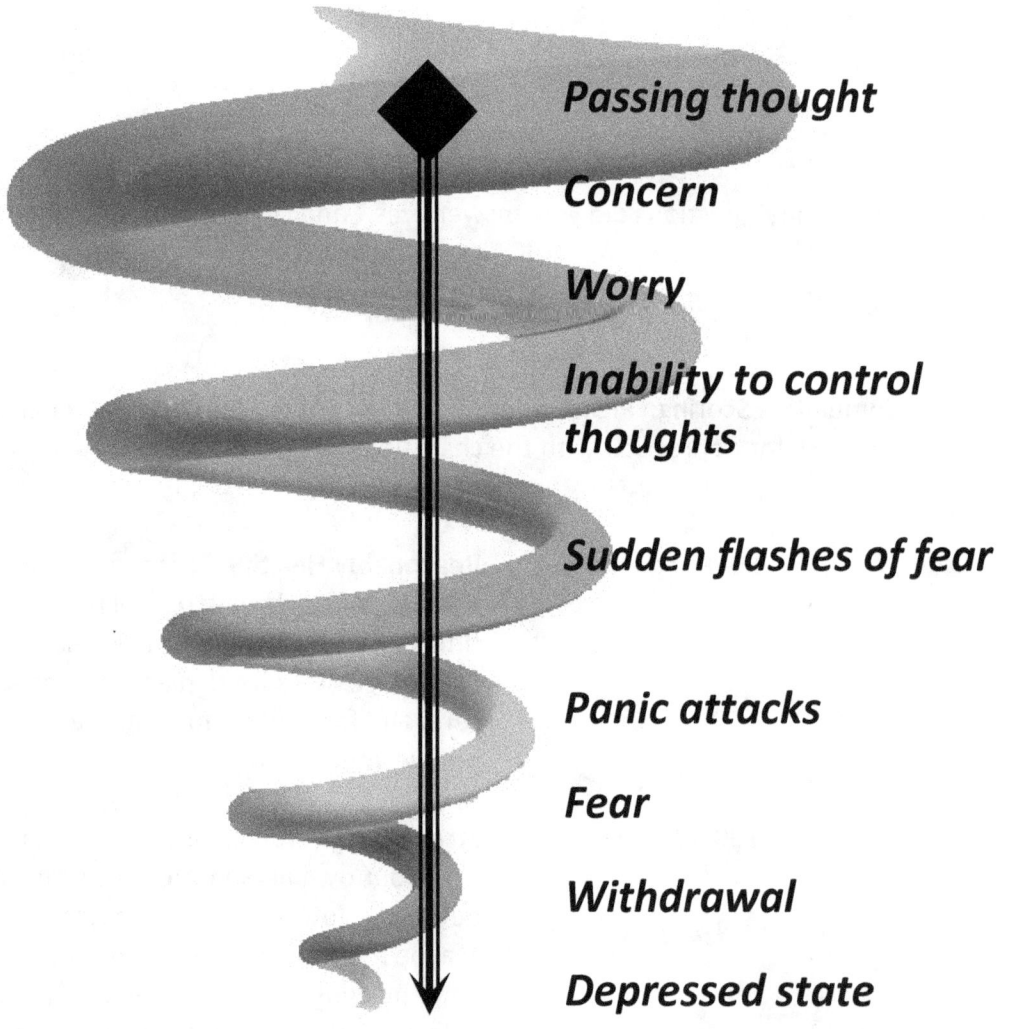

- Passing thought
- Concern
- Worry
- Inability to control thoughts
- Sudden flashes of fear
- Panic attacks
- Fear
- Withdrawal
- Depressed state

Section Five
The Counselor's Role in the Healing Journey

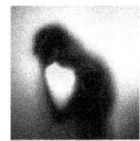

The recurring origins of Depression in our culture are varied: stress, emotional pain, loss, trauma, physical body changes to name a few. Over the years, I have discovered that there are several keys in helping clients deal with the realities of Depression.

1. **Medication.** If a client is struggling with the temptation to hurt him or herself; or if that client is contemplating hurting another human being, you are absolutely required to refer them to a physician, with the recommendation they be placed on an anti-anxiety medications, or an anti-depressants. If the person is in crisis, it is usually more than appropriate to call 911, or send them to the nearest hospital or Urgent Care. If medication is prescribed, it customarily provided for short-term use, in order to enable the client to work through the issues presenting themselves at the present time. If Depression is a biological issue, the person may be prescribed medications for a much longer season of time. (It is important to ask the client to see their medical physician, or a psychiatrist in order to assess their medical need for an anti-depressant). Never, never, *ever* diagnose a client's medical issues.

2. **Comfort or Change?** The first step in dealing with Depression is that a client become aware of their need to choose to become healthy. In reality, this decision is a choice for change. In contrast, as long as a person remains in a place of demanding those who surround them give comfort only, they will never be able to move forward.

3. **Set a Sensitive Pace.** Never overwhelm a client with too much information. Each step in the healing process is a step the person must make, howbeit supported, on their own. There are no shortcuts to healing. Allow time for the client to discover, absorb, apply, and review. It is important in the walk of a disciple that a person become equipped during the healing process, to understand what God is doing.

4. **Ownership.** A client must take ownership of the Training will help the client come to that point. It is important The most important key in equipping a client to deal effectively with symptoms of Depression is helping them become willing to embrace personal ownership of the catalysts for their depression. By this, I am referring to choices they have made, perspectives they have believed, and attitudes they have allowed to become unchangeable.

5. **Community.** In my own experience, people who suffer from Depression usually have difficulty being around other people. Even though they don't really want to be alone, they have learned to become comfortable with their sense of isolation. Usually, this type of depression carries with it a history of broken trust issues, which must be addressed and processed if the client is to move forward in their personal development. Depending upon the readiness of a client to move forward, it can help to schedule two appointment in a week's time, as well as enlist the help of family members to support the reprogramming of the person's attachment/trust skills in relationships.

There are many causes for Depression:

Biological and genetic background
Environmental factors
Grief/Loss
Abuse
Failure
Chemical imbalances in the brain
Hormonal changes
Isolation/Abandonment

*Helping a client take apart their anger issues, can also become
a tool in helping them to decipher and dismantle their Depression.*

Anger's Path

Life Approach Attitude (model/imprinting)	The Message Believed (about self) (activator/trigger)	First Emotion (below the surface)	Secondary Emotion (evident behavior)
Everyone should just be nice and get along.	People should listen when I tell them how to get along.	Hurt; Fear of Rejection Fear of Conflict	ANGER
My life should be easier than it is.	Life should be fair; Others should take care of me.	Exclusion; Justice Frustration; Insecurity	ANGER
I need everyone to respect/like me.	There is something wrong with me.	Rejection: Disapproval Shame; Confusion	ANGER
I should be in control of what happens in my life.	Other people should allow me to have the control.	Fear of Vulnerability Fear of Rejection	ANGER
I should always know what to do when bad things happen in my life.	I don't know what to do in this situation. I am relationally un-tooled.	Embarrassment Fear of Rejection Fear of Being Known	ANGER
I should always be "on top" of things	I can't meet the expectations I have/others have.	Shame; Helplessness Self-Hatred	ANGER
Mistakes/Failings are unacceptable.	If I fail, or am wrong, I am unacceptable.	Fear of Disapproval Abandonment; Self-Hatred	ANGER
I should use my skills, and not do things I feel are beneath me.	Others should do the things I don't want to do for me.	Entitlement Improper Self-Image	ANGER
I should never make mistakes.	I cannot be wrong, or apologize/admit weakness.	Pride; Entitlement;Confusion Shame; Fear of Vulnerability	ANGER
I have to earn my way.	My value is determined by what I know how to do.	Overwhelmed; Fear of Rejection; Self-rejection; Guilt; Futility	ANGER

(Between columns 1 and 2: CONFLICT OCCURS)

©2010 dg/atg

Required Choices to Heal

Where do you see yourself on the scale?

In order for a client to have motivation to partner with what
he or she is learning in the healing process, it
is vitally important they be able to
identify where they feel they are living in
regard to the struggle they are experiencing.

The practice of taking time for to help a client make identification
and placement of personal issues has served well to help the person
take "ownership" of their part in the growth journey.

Sometimes, I create a little chart like the one below, to help a person realize
What our goals are….and then, I am able to present the challenge:
"Are you willing to partner with me to come to a healthy place?"

Anxious   Afraid   Depressed

The Role of a Client's Regrets
(in Dealing with Depression)

It is not unusual for a depressed client to look back over their relationships and choices, especially in the midst of grieving a painful loss. In fact, isn't it something we all do whenever something in our lives goes the wrong way?

Then, in the midst of looking back, it is a scheme of Hell to mire a person into focusing on all of their perceived failures.

It has been said many times that in Life, our hindsight is always perfect; "20/20." But then, the difficulty with perfect "sight" is that we each tend to judge our *past* selves based upon our *present* knowing.

We do this without even thinking about it.

And then, we tend to believe that everyone else also knew way back then what we have just become aware of and now understand. We enter into conflict with ourselves, and listen to Self-hatred. We inwardly condemn and judge our efforts, based on assumed knowledge which may or may not have been true at all.

And, true or not, it is certainly outside of our control....

Regret is an emotion. That is all it is.

However, that being said; Regret is a *powerful* emotion. It can deceive, steal identity, highjack value and esteem, enslave motives, and drive a person; to suicide, or at the least, to violate personal values.

Regret is an accusation against our imperfections. What were we *thinking?* Why didn't we do *then* what we would do *now?*

One of the things I enjoy being allowed to do as a Christian counselor, is to remind people of the nature of Abba Father. I love to read Psalm 103 to them, and ask them to memorize verses 8-14. I love to watch people learn to receive the forgiveness and Grace of God – and allow that forgiveness and Grace into their own hearts; no longer arguing with God about whether they "deserve" to be forgiven.

Years ago, I worked with a woman who was walking away from a failed marriage. In the midst of protecting the futures of her children, and securing her own physical and emotional state, she constantly dealt with Regret. In my own view, she had stayed longer with her abuser than she really should have. Co-dependent, she absorbed responsibilities not her own. What should she have done differently? How could she have ensured a different outcome? She felt she had lost her purpose.

She was depressed.

When her "Denial Bubble" finally burst, her Present Reality became evident. Then, surprisingly, her level of Regret increased. I think sharing some of her inner thought patterns will help you to understand how powerfully this emotion works to undermine personal purpose and identity.

We spoke in sessions. We spoke on the telephone. One night, she sent me an email. And I wanted to share a version of it with you, and my response. (Names and specifics have been changed to maintain confidentiality.)

Debbye:

You asked about my regrets. As I've thought about it, I am overwhelmed with them. Before, I was thinking just about my regrets over getting the kids out of there and about getting out of there myself. But now, I have regrets about so many other things....

So here are my regrets....

- *Spending all of my adult life without knowing the love of a good man*
- *Not leaving him when he first abused our son*
- *Marrying three abusers*
- *That I ever became involved with him*
- *That I gave him sex at all. He destroyed my hope of relationship*
- *That I have never known a healthy family*
- *That I didn't fight for all that I saw I needed.*
- *That I didn't fight for all the kids needed.*
- *That I didn't tell any of them I wanted proper treatment for me and the kids*
- *That I didn't confront his addictions*
- *That I didn't confront his problems with money*

Here are the regrets that carry the greatest pain for me:

- *I moved away from family*
- *I missed the births of my grandchildren*
- *I have missed the birthdays of my grandchildren*
- *I have nothing to show for my life*

Here are the regrets that carry even greater pain for me:

- *I am alone – again. Will I always be alone?*
- *I am too old*
- *I am afraid of sex; I am afraid of no more sex*
- *Fear of sex; fear of no more sex*
- *Everywhere I go, people come in twos. I am always longing for it.*
- *I am painfully aware of what I am lacking. I dwell on it.*
- *I am frustrated and angry and regretful.*
- *I do not want him, nor do I regret leaving him. I just regret the hole it has put in my life.*
- *I don't know how to let Jesus fill it up.*
- *The threat to me is that it will always be a hole.*

I say to myself how shallow this existence is; it is self-consuming and lacks value when compared to greater things such as growing in the Lord or serving others. So I am ashamed of these longings.

I realize the futility of these thoughts. I know that my future depends more on healing than filling the hole. But its hard. I want to focus on being a whole woman just as I am. But I can't and am constantly threatened that this is all there is.

I know that Truth is with me, but threats stare me down. Will I will be alone and sad always? Or I will marry again and find the same failure in marriage as I have already experienced.. again? Or maybe I don't deserve to have another marriage. Or a good man won't want me and will never be available anyway because he is already married…

So this preoccupation with men is really bad. I need help to fix this.

Here is my reply:

Hey girl –

Thanks for your vulnerability… I know this must be difficult….

There is nothing wrong with the need for relationship. It is what we are created for – and you've never had to process this stuff before. It's kind of built up on you, you know? Most of what you feel is absolutely normal.

You don't need to be ashamed of having longings. Part of learning to accept ourselves and the Lord's love for us involves being able to admit the needs and yearnings we feel. So, it might be a good idea to write out a description of what you wish your life looked like right now.

What does it feel like you're missing? Make a list. Nothing is too small to consider.

Looking at the email... There is a lot of grief in these regrets – and most of it has to do with the fear of being alone – even the marriages before this one.

So here are a couple of questions to help in the growth process...

How long has the hole really been there? Adulthood? Teens? Childhood?

What messages were received in your heart – that then became perceptions about your own value as you got older – to the point that you thought that only an abusive someone with an addiction would want you?

Did you realize at the time that you were settling? Or were you just happy to have someone say they cared for you?

These are hard questions, but they need answers.

The hole is as deep as it is because it goes back a long way – my suspicion is that the hole has been there since the rejection issues we discussed in your childhood took place.

The regrets are just the face on the real need – We tend to put weight on the people we choose because we think they will fill our places of need. I think this is what happened with the hubbies you ended up with – you hoped they would become the source to fix the pain from your girlhood – but it became more of the same --

Regrets are the emotions that tell us we made a wrong choice.

And let me say that I don't think all of this is shallow and self-consumed – you are on a quest for healing. We are committed to the process, and you won't ever be really alone again.

I don't think that another man at the moment would bring healing either...... perhaps that is why you are hearing the Lord's voice more these days. I do think it your emotions might viewed as an invitation from the Lord to spend a little more time in contemplation with Him.... because He is where the real healing and answers are –

But then, because He is not tangible – it can also be threatening. We all long for physical touch...... that might be why it is painful to worship, or to spend time in the Word......

It feels dark right now. And there are lots of avenues that could be an escape from what you feel.... I'm so glad you have discovered that truth, and are making solid choices. These moments are a season, and are not permanent. No matter what pathway you choose next, we both know it cannot become a hiding place from the real growth sources.....

It's clear you know that – so please know this is my feeble attempt to encourage you and remind you how far you have come. If you are going to walk out of this place, it will take the kind of healthy thinking you are learning now. It will take a decision to intentionally apply new ways of thinking about yourself, your purpose, and the Lord's plan for you.......

Please call me – We'll look for a healthy way to help you walk through this particular shade of blackness – so you don't lose yourself in there ----

We both know a Big Guy with a bright flashlight!! (lol)

You are loved, my friend. You have more value than you know.

Deb

**People don't care how much you know....
Until they know how much you care.**

John Maxwell

Walking a Client Through Forgiveness

When a person battles through Depression, one of the mechanisms feeding the cycling problem is the human tendency to relive experienced past wounding. One of the main steps in the healing journey is the person coming into willingness to forgive.

In the biblical languages, the word "forgive" is the English word, translated from Hebrew and Greek root words which mean "release," or "let go." Forgiveness then, is a person's willingness to release the individual or group of individuals who hurt them. Without forgiveness, an inky black root of Bitterness begins to tap down into the soul. In Hebrews 12:15, the writer urges believers to "looking carefully lest anyone fall short of the grace of God; lest any root of bitterness springing up cause trouble, and by this many become defiled."

Bitterness then, can be caused in a life, when a person does not apply the Grace of God to the wound experienced; only God's Grace can change something bitter into something sweet.

Forgiveness cannot happen flippantly; nor can it take place simply because we want to show ourselves to be dutiful and obedience disciples. It cannot happen devoid of emotion.

Forgiveness is a process. It is a choice which does not happen all at once. The one doing the forgiving must grieve the loss caused by the injury. As the wound is faced, and taken apart, its depth assessed and laid on the sacrificial altar before God, the wounded person then is able to release their injurer with full knowledge of what they are releasing.

This is how closure occurs in the life.

Forgiveness is the means through which we are able to experience reconciliation within the members of our soul. When we pursue the process of becoming able to release another from the debt they owe us, we pursue the core purpose of the discipleship method. We become like Christ Jesus.

Forgiveness is not healing. Many times, we confuse the two, somehow thinking if we just "choose" without emotion, we can shortcut the process. But then we struggle with anger, self-hatred, guilt, and ultimately Depression.

Experiencing the longer pathway allows us to separate the two progressions. Just as a person has to go to the doctor when they experience a stab wound, so a wounded soul must be intentionally assessed, addressed, and brought to a healthy state; many times utilizing therapy and exercises for emotional development.

The journey to forgive the person who wielded the knife, however, is much different. To forgive means giving up the right to keep track of what is owed to us. It means divesting the blame and injustice we feel into the heart and hands of a loving God. He is the Keeper of the Accounts. In Him, everything comes into balance. In fact, the Greek word "logos," which is translated "Word" in John 1:1, is actually a bookkeeping term. It refers to the figures which bring balance to the accounts.

Jesus is the Logos. When we divest our right to hold others accountable, He brings the Balance.

He will always be the Last Word.

On the next few pages, is a set of worksheets I developed to help clients who are walking through the decision to forgive injuries they have experienced. The worksheets are taken from a program for women available through our ministry called, "Ruth and Naomi – The Healing Journey." The workbook is designed to accompany twelve mp3 sessions; both are available through our ministry offices.

God's Balance Sheet of Forgiveness
(adapted from "Ruth and Naomi: The Healing Journey," Chapter 10)

1. Please turn to Matthew 18:21-35. Read the story, and then answer the questions below.

    a. verse 23   Who was responsible to settle the accounts?

    b. verse 24-25 The first slave owed more than $10 million in silver to his master. Even if he and his family were separated and sold, the price they would draw could not come anywhere close to that much. (In earthly terms, the man owed more than his life was worth.)

    c. verse 26   Could the slave pay the debt, in reality?

    d. verse 27   What were the steps of forgiveness, the king walked through? List them here.

    1.

    2.

    3.

2. Read verse 28. The second servant's debt was the equivalent of one day's wage. What blind spot did the first servant have?

    Could he see the relationship between the debt the second servant owed him, and his own debt that had been forgiven?

a. verse 29-30 Was the first servant's heart open to the man who owed him the debt of one day's wage?

b. Was he grateful, really, for his own debt being forgiven?

How can you tell?

c. What would have shown his gratefulness?

d. Read verse 31-25. How does the king view the first servant's injustice in his dealings?

3. What did the king consider to have been a better representation of the king's action and attitude toward indebtedness?

4. What is the end result of the first slave's attitude of unforgiveness?

a. What areas in your own life have experienced torment? List them here.

5. Copy verse 35 here.

6. Take a few moments to journal on a separate piece of paper regarding painful memories and experiences in your past that seem to be "speaking" to you lately.

7. From that journal, please utilize the next few pages and make a list of the injuries, which have been speaking to your soul, and have been "in your face," in regard to pain and trust issues. Please make a bulleted list of those injuries in the left hand column below. Please also name the person who inflicted the injury with the memory, or painful circumstance. If the injury was due to a choice which you made, please list yourself as the person who inflicted injury.

Injuries	Contrast assignment

Injuries	Contrast assignment

Injuries	Contrast assignment

8. Our own pain tends to blind us to the needs of others. And our pain is based upon our perception of the situation. Our perceptions are the basis of our reactions and choices.

It is important that we realize that we are not alone – ever. That even when things happen to us that were not the best possible situation – that when we bring that pain and difficulty to Father God, He is able to bring good out of it. He is able to heal. In order to facilitate that process – we must let go of our own perceptions, and allow Him to give us fresh insight and understanding.

Please look up the following scriptures, and please contrasting character qualities that pertain to Father God in the "Contrast Assignment" column, as they relate to the injuries you have listed.

The Scriptures are:

I Corinthians 13

Psalm 103

Psalm 91

Psalm 54:4-5

Psalm 18

Ephesians 2:1-10

9. Meet with a prayer partner and walk through these areas of pain and difficulty, making confession of your heart attitude, and any struggles you may have with releasing the injustices of these situations.

10. Ask your mentor to help you to understand what bondages and difficulties the person who hurt you might have been struggling with, and ask the Lord to give you compassion for them. This is the first step in learning to forgive.

General Prayer for Freedom

Father God, I acknowledge you as my heavenly Father. I understand and believe what the Word of God says about your nature.

Earthly men may hate me, but You love me. Earthly men may seek to violate and control me, but you will never violate my will. Earthly men may have abused me, but I know that there is no end to your mercy and love for me. I know that you desire to make my paths straight, and to bless me. You do not reward me according to my sins, but according to Your own righteousness.

I have a purpose in Your eyes, and You want me to know and understand that purpose. You want to be my strength when I am weak. You want to be my refuge and to deliver me from all evil. You want me to trust in You and be helped.

So, Father God, I choose today, to surrender to Yom will for my life. I choose to be obedient to You. I choose to obey the authority figures you have put into my life. I know they must give account for my soul.

Lord Jesus, I acknowledge and accept Your gift of life for me. Thank you for the provision of your Blood, which is eternal and all powerful, and has no limits in its availability to me. I apply that Blood to my heart and my life. I repent for allowing the influences and powers of darkness to acquire my allegiance. Please forgive me for listening to those voices and giving in to them. Please wash away the false security which has deceived my heart into forsaking You when seeking love and comfort.

Please melt away those chains which I have allowed to overtake my heart. I repent for seeking comfort and escape anywhere but through Your provision of love for me. I turn away from self-reliance and trusting my own flesh, and the flesh of others to guide me. I choose to trust You. I choose to trust Your word to be the complete counsel for my life.

I choose to disregard any suspicious nature which the enemy of my soul, the devil, uses against me to accuse or condemn those You have put in my path to help and bless me and bring me into freedom. I surrender my desire to be in control of my deliverance. I choose to follow with an open and listening heart.

Father, I confess my fear to you. I am afraid of being violated when my walls are taken down. I am afraid the process of destruction will begin all over again. But I know these are threats from the kingdom of darkness, and so I ask for your Perfect love to cast out fear in me in regard to my freedom. Please be the strength of my life and my shield. Please be the strong high tower into which I can run for safety. You are my Helper.

I want to become the person you created me to be.

I acknowledge you as the Restorer of my soul, and I recognize that Satan has stolen from me my purpose, he has lied to me and brought death and destruction to my heart, life and mind.

I hate him with a perfect hatred. I will not allow demonic voices to give me a false sense of security and identity. I choose to hear Your voice, Father God. Please speak to me.

Holy Spirit, I release You within my heart, and I give you full permission to make my life and person a holy and pure vessel for your habitation.

Thank you Lord that you love me. I am your child. I choose Your way.

Prayer to help in Releasing Forgiveness

Father God, thank you for your love for me. I know that you love me unconditionally. I choose to walk in Your ways. Thank you for the gift of your Son, Who died so that I might live forever.

Father, I choose to forgive everyone who has knowingly and unknowingly inflicted hurts and bruises upon my life.

With my will, I will forgive, and I trust You to fill my heart with your love and the feelings of forgiveness in the days to come.

Father, I choose to release my rights to hold on to these hurts and bruises. I choose to confess them to you, and allow you to be the vindicator and Healer of my Heart.

Thank you for your peace. In Jesus' name, Amen.

The Spiritual Significance of An Apology

"And I will give them one heart, and put a new spirit within them. And I will take the heart of stone out of their flesh and give them a heart of flesh, that they may walk in My statutes and keep My ordinances and do them. Then they will be My people, and I shall be their God." Ezek. 11:18-20

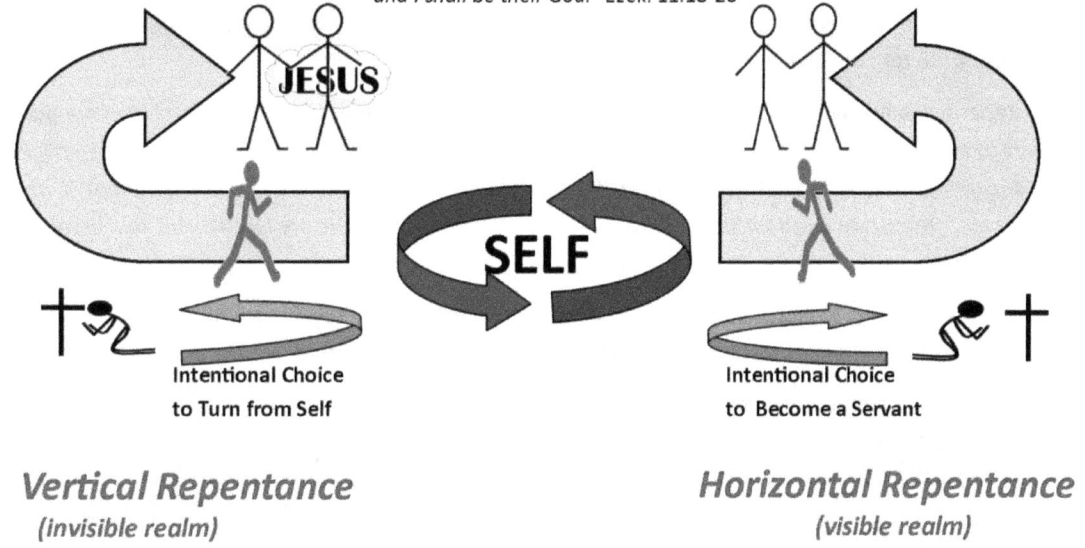

Intentional Choice to Turn from Self

Intentional Choice to Become a Servant

Vertical Repentance
(invisible realm)

Horizontal Repentance
(visible realm)

Four Statements in the Healthy Apology
Healthy Apologies are essential in building Relationships

Note: *A true apology is offered whether the other person is ready to reciprocate or not. Also, a true apology does not hold elements of, "I will if you will." When we repent to another person, we do so for the sake of the relationship, because we feel before God it is the right thing to do.*

1. "I'm sorry."
We take ownership of our regret, and express our regret over our actions/words to the person who has experienced damaged relationship with us.

2. "I was wrong."
We acknowledge our lack of perfection, and communicate that we made a mistake in the relationship. To take this to its healthiest/deepest level, the "I was wrong statement" should also include the relational territory violated. For example: "I was wrong to speak to you that way," or "I was wrong to embarrass you in front of your friends."

3. "Would you please forgive me?"
We express our desire to continue the relationship, by requesting forgiveness. When we do, we realize that the other person is not immediately required to release us from the offense. In cases of deeper wounding, the ability to forgive might take time for the person to discover. If we try to apologize without forgiveness taking place, we short-circuit the relationship and make it totally one-sided; we avoid the real work of relating well – avoiding inevitable conflict. When we ask for forgiveness, it is a good practice to add the instance to the end of the question as well. Such as "Would you please forgive me for sending you that signal? I would never want to hurt you that way again, even unintentionally."

4. "What can I do to make things right between us?"
This statement sets a foundation for the healing work of restitution to take place. When we take ownership of our mistakes in relationship, seeking reconciliation and restoration, usually it will require a short period of re-building trust with the person we have injured. This process takes time, and effort.

Vertical Repentance — *(invisible realm, eternal, spiritual)*

1. **When we repent, we are apologizing to God.** *An apology involves more than feeling sorry or regretful over our behavior, or fearful of experiencing the consequences we have earned. The Biblical word translated "repent" from the original language is "metanoeo," which means "to change the way we think, and to amend behaviors." In modern terms, it means "to turn around," or "make a U-turn." (Luke 15:10 and 17:10)*

2. **Repentance involves taking responsibility for our behaviors.** *When we take ownership of our actions, it involves recognizing those areas where we have stepped away from the embrace and relationship of God. Part of this process is the understanding of our own weaknesses in being tempted. James wrote that we are tempted when we are "drawn away." The Greek word for this concept is "exelko," meaning that we are lured away, and break the embrace of relationship. (James 1:4)*

3. **When we repent to God, we are told to admit to Him what we have done wrong. When we do, it opens the door for God's forgiveness in our lives, and begins the process of cleansing and healing our hearts.** *(I John 1:9)*

4. **Maintaining a repentant heart, and seeking to keep our hearts open and soft, keeps us in a healthy place of being in right relationship with God.** *(righteousness= right relationship with God.)*

Horizontal Repentance — *(visible realm, eternal, spiritual)*

1. **When we apologize to another person, we are repenting for sinning against them.** *An apology given to another person is not just saying, "I'm sorry." In a shadow of the power of an apology to God, an apology given to another person, also involves more than feeling sorry or regretful over our behavior, or fearful of experiencing the consequences we have earned. (Ephesians 4:22-32)*

2. **It takes humility to apologize.** *A true apology is more concerned with the damage our actions and/or words have caused in the other person, than we are with clarifying or blaming someone/something for our behaviors. It is more concerned with seeking to understand, than it is with seeking to be understood. When we allow our hearts to become hardened towards another person, we succumb to the deception of Pride, protecting our own rights and sense of entitlement. (James 4:6-10)*

3. **Positional authority is temporary. Relational equity is eternal.** *Our relationships and personal life-lessons, are the only entities we can take with us into the eternal realm. When we defend our image, our position, our rights, or our opinions we develop hardness of heart that separates us from relationship — first with others, then with God. (Romans 12:3-10, I John 4:7-11, Matthew 5:21-25)*

4. **We are called to treat each other the way we would treat Christ Jesus.** *(Matthew 25:31-46)*

5. **An apology opens the door to the process of forgiveness, cleansing, restoration of relationship with another person, and emotional healing. There can be no depth of relationship without the willingness to admit mistakes, misunderstandings and/or failures. We are called to see ourselves as servants of others, rather than seeking to have our rights satisfied.** *(Galatians 5:13-14, Luke 22:24-27, Philippians 2:3-15)*

6. **An apology is only the beginning place for communication and healing to take place.**

The Principles of Change

1. There is always hope for change.

2. We cannot change what we do not acknowledge.

3. The primary ingredient of the change process is Truth (in love) in an open heart.

4. We cannot change others. We can only change ourselves.

5. Repentance is the only catalyst (beginning place) for change to occur.

6. Our inner brokenness is the beginning place for repentance, and therefore Change.

7. Changes we seek to make within ourselves without the help of the Holy Spirit, will never be permanent, because they are based in our own works and effort.

8. We cannot expect God to give grace or healing, when we are unwilling to repent.

9. Growth cannot happen without change.

10. Change will involve both forward and backward motion, always with our eyes fixed upon the goal of becoming like Christ.

11. The Doorway into the Change Process is guarded from the inside, by a person who must open the door from the inside. It cannot be forced open.

12. Change must be chosen, sometimes with struggle.

13. Change comes as a result of Training, not as a result of simply trying, using the same tools we have used in the past.

14. Change is a process. It takes time. What took years to tear down will require a season of hard work to redeem, repair and restore.

15. It takes intentional maintenance for change to remain.

©atg/dcg

Learning the Ten Phases of Handling Depression

Phase One Take a personal assessment of the state you are living in right now. What signs are there that it's time for a change? Write down the signs, and make a list of the change you sense is needed. Speak with a medical professional regarding the possible temporary need for an anti-depressant medication.

Phase Two Is it possible that you are angry, and not just depressed? What are you angry about? In which relationships in your life do you find it difficult to share what you really feel? What decisions can you make that would help you to make the changes you discovered were needed in Step One?

Phase Three It's time to accept the value your Creator has placed upon your life. It is not a sin to be sincerely honest about the difficulties you are experiencing right now. It is healthy to be able to share those difficulties with someone you trust. Why not seek help from a professional counselor? Or at least speak with a friend whose advice you have proven to be helpful in the past?

Phase Four Has depression become a habit for you? Have you allowed your heart to be defined by it? Is it your "safe place?" Take time to consider why that might be the case. Are there undeveloped areas of your personality style, which might be manifesting through depression?

Phase Five Let yourself fully grieve your losses. Celebrate the Life Lessons you are learning. Yield anew to the Holy Spirit's processes on a daily basis.

Phase Six Let go of your need to control others. Resolve to accept your limits, and seek to control only those things inside your control; namely just you.

Phase Seven Make a decision to strengthen your inner self; that is, the vulnerable and emotionally un-tooled part of your personhood. Choose to let go of past injuries and abuses where you have allowed those situations to label and define your identity. Work to discover who you have been created to become.

Phase Eight Choose to allow other people into your life. Share your fears, and any temptations you may have felt about suicide, or dying. Allow those safe and trustworthy people to comfort you; without draining them. When someone proves to be untrustworthy (and people do), it is appropriate to limit your sharing with that person, while not closing your heart toward that person.

Phase Nine Listen and choose to consider the truths you are learning in this new place of community, even if it is painful, or difficult to do so. Learning of an area needing change in your life is not a place of rejection. Rather, it is an opportunity to discover a place of needed growth and healing. Choose to become a respond-er rather than a react-er.

Phase Nine Become committed to having positive words to say in response to negative ones. Become a cheerleader for the people within your sphere of influence.

Phase Ten Resolve to become a life-long learner. Many times, depression has to do with a sense of being forgotten and abandoned. When we choose to re-enter the lives of those people who are already around us, we learn very important experiential truths regarding ourselves, our relationships with others, and our relationship with God.

> "As long as I was running away from God, I pursued the things that I saw to be in the light, rather than pursuing the light. When I turned away from those things, and I turned to God, I realized what was really important. I saw God for who He is, and then I saw the truth about myself."   Augustine

Section Six
What the Bible teaches about Depression

"I cannot know myself until I know God."   John Calvin

In Proverbs 12:25, the Bible says, "Heaviness in the heart of man makes it stoop; but a good word makes it glad." (KJV)

When we take this scripture apart, in order to understand the meaning of the original language (ancient Hebrew), we make a startling discovery.

Heaviness	= de-agah	meaning –	*anxiety, anxious care, dread*
Heart	= leb	meaning –	*the soul, the midst, the seat of emotion/passion*
Stoop	= shachah	meaning –	*to depress, to bow down under a weight*
Good	= towb	meaning -	*good, pleasant, appropriate, ethical, of good understanding*
Word	= dabar	meaning -	*speech, utterance, saying*
Glad	= samach	meaning -	*to cause to rejoice, to make glad, joyful, or merry*

If we re-read the verse, with a more exact translation of the original language, it reads like this:

"Anxiety and dread in the midst of a person's soul causes depression and a bowing down under a weight; but an appropriate and understanding saying will cause them to become glad, and to rejoice."

The Bible also refers to Depression as a "Spirit of Heaviness."

Exposing the Spirit of Heaviness
(commonly referred to as depression)

Within Scripture there are several words which are translated "heaviness" in the English language. In researching this subject, I have pulled most instances of each Hebrew word~ appearance in the Old Testament text, and done a cross-reference with the New Testament Greek text where possible. ("#" symbols indicate Strong's Concordance reference numbers)

Depending upon the difficulty/bruise encountered, the spirit of heaviness seems to have varying degrees of intensity. I have listed the variations in what I personally understood to be the order in which they occur in the human soul.

Layer One

keheh (kay-heh) — It means to be faint-hearted, weak, lacking color, dull and dark. This word is translated as "smoking" in Isaiah 42:3. It means "to falter, and be restrained"

#3544 (Hebrew, Strong's Concordance numbering)

This word occurs in:

a) Lev. 13:6.21.26.28.39. and 56 in regard to leprosy. It is translated "dark". When the skin begins to appear dark, or have its surface falter, then the diagnosis is leprosy. *Thought: Is a spirit of heaviness the beginning of a "leprosy" in the human soul?*

b) Isaiah 42:3. It is translated "smoking" --the verse says "a smoking flax he will not put out". This indicates that Father God is a merciful God who knows when someone has been quenched and is faint, or faltering and in difficulty. He will bring back the flame to its full intensity, rather than pass down a harsh verdict.

c) Isaiah 61:3. It is translated "heaviness". This verse not only gives the identity for what process is beginning in the human soul, but it also gives one of the antidotes for depression. The verse says .."to put on a garment of praise for the spirit of heaviness." (To put on a garment of praise requires the active participation of the person under attack. It also could mean an immersion, in a sense, in praise –via filling the atmosphere with praise and worship music which they actively join in with, etc.)

Layer Two

da'agah (deh-aw-gaw) It means carefulness, fear, heaviness with care, anxiety or anxious care

#1674 (Hebrew, Strong's Concordance numbering)

This word occurs in:

a) Joshua 22:4 and is translated "fear"; A careful and anxious fear creates a heaviness which stops a person from moving into new areas and taking action. Most people in this stage are becoming passive observers.

b) Proverbs 12:25 and is translated "Heaviness". The verse reads "Heaviness in the heart of man maketh it stoop". The phrase "maketh it stoop", is better translated from the Hebrew as "brings depression".

c) Jeremiah 49:23 and is translated "sorrow". This indicates it is a sorrow and faint-hearted-ness, which actually speaks to a person. That means by not letting go of the heaviness, a person is actually opening the ears of their heart to the voices of the demonic realm.

d) Ezekiel 4:16./ 12:18-19 and is translated "care", as well as "carefulness". It denotes an inability to enjoy even the simple things of life such as a meal, due to the weight and worry of the cares surrounding them.

Antidote for this layer: Recognizing that fear enters into the heart at this point. Life no longer can be observed without fear's interpretation and ever-present "what if". In I Peter 5:7 we are instructed to "cast all of our cares (Greek-- *merinma* -- cares and anxiety) upon Him who cares for us". The Greek word *merinma* denotes a distraction upon the soul. We are to put our eyes upon Jesus and look to Him and not to the threats and difficulties around us. I John 4:18 says *"Perfect love cast out fear".* The person needs an understanding of the perfect and unconditional love of God. *(Requires an inner revelation.)*

Layer Three

tuwgab (too-gab)   It means to hold grief, heaviness or sorrow

#8424 (Hebrew, Strong's Concordance numbering)

This word occurs in:

a) Psalm 119:28 and is translated "heaviness". The verse says "My soul melteth for heaviness: strengthen thou me according unto Thy Word." (There is a melting process which has begun within the soul. Hope, Joy, Rational Thought, etc. begin to be melted away, and a heavy sorrow is put in its place.) The answer for this is the active partaking of the truth of the Word --especially in relationship to the Father's plans for the person's life. (Jeremiah 29:11 is a key promise here).

b) Proverbs 10: 1 and Proverbs 17:21 indicate that a parent can come to this point of depression due to a child's errant behavior and rebellion.

c) Proverbs 14: 13 describes the heart of the depressed person. No ability to laugh without sorrow being present.

#2726 (Greek)   katepheia (kat-ay-fi-ah)   It means to carry a downcast look, to be full of shame, dejection, and gloom

This word occurs in:

a) James 4:9 and is translated "heaviness". The verse is part of a segment (verses 6-10) which addresses those who are too proud in heart to admit they need God's cleansing.

#3076 (Greek)   lupeo (loo-peh-o)   It means to be sorrowful, to grieve, to be in heaviness, to be offended or to be uneasy because scruples have been violated. It is a word which seems to be used in connection with the emotions as opposed to a spiritual difficulty.

This word occurs in:

a) **Matthew 14:9** and is translated "sorry". Herod felt a heaviness when he was forced to give his wife's daughter John the Baptist's head on a platter.

b) **Matthew 19:22** and is translated "sorry". The rich young lawyer was heavy of heart (but was unwilling) to give up what he had to follow Jesus. What God wanted went against his self-will.

c) **Mark 14:19** and is translated "sorrowful". The disciples responded in this attitude when Jesus told them that one of them would betray Him. Self-will was unwilling to admit that any of the twelve would become that sinful.

d) **John 21:17** and is translated "grieved". Peter was grieved when Jesus asked a third time "Do you love me?". It offended his self-will to think that maybe he didn't love Jesus as much as he thought he did.

e) **Ephesians 4:30** and is translated "grieve". We are told that the Holy Spirit can be grieved by our lack of response or our disobedience to His ministry. It grieves Him when we follow our self-will.

f) **I Peter 1:6** and is translated "heaviness". The verse says "Wherein ye greatly rejoice, though now for a season if need be, ye are in heaviness through manifold temptations." When self-will is tempted to sin, and we resist, we are told to rejoice in that strength, because it is only for a temporary season. A depressed person has difficulty believing that the particular season they are experiencing could be temporary. Many depressed people consider making a permanent end to a temporary problem.

#916 (Greek) bareo (bar-eh-o) It means to be heavy, to be pressed down (by something else), to be burdened, or under a charge, to weigh down or depress (has a tone of violence and unsparing cruelty) an encumbrance

This word occurs in:

a) <u>II Corinthians 1:8</u> and is translated "pressed out" The phrase in which it is used says ".. that we were pressed out of measureth above strength insomuch that we despaired even of life." This indicates that the burden imposed upon the depressed individual separates them from the desire to continue living. All they can feel is the weight they are carrying.

b) <u>II Corinthians 5:4</u> and is translated "being burdened". The idea is conveyed through the verse that rather than be affected passively by what is seeking to oppress, the desire should be that our morality (grk="thnetos", literally the "ability to die") be swallowed up in life. Take the offensive before it gets any worse!!

Antidote for this Layer: Memorization of key verses of the Word of God, which deal directly with the areas of the person's life under attack. Daily quotation of the Word of God, which will edify, and build up, that which has been broken and melted down. *(It also helps to realize that the person's eyes are focused upon themselves and their difficulty, rather than on the Lord, His love and His ability to heal their problem.)*

Note for Understanding: The Word of God is very dear in James 1:13 that God does not tempt us. The reason for the depth of the depression at this point comes from the person's stubborn holding on to their tangible understandings. They have given in to the temptation to trust their own abilities, or those abilities of" qualified professionals" to set them free. Many times, deliverance is made more complex- as drugs and world-based therapies are added to the mix, and the person becomes even more insecure and confused --now leaning on what can be a mind and mood altering drug which only mask the problem.

Satan has stolen their song, and the desire to worship God in an active sense lies passive within them. They have chosen to hold on to the grief rather than submit it to the Lord and ask for His healing. At this point, usually the person manifests many attention-getting qualities, but never seems to come to a solution of the problem The problem seems to change from day to day, and they just can't seem to find out what is really wrong. A person in this state is typically led by their emotions, and spends very little time in prayer. It took a long time to get to this point, and the victory is a sure one, but because it is so entrenched in their habit patterns and personality, it takes time to peel away the "layers" of oppression.

Layer Four

#3077 (Greek) Lupe (loo-pay) a sorrow which is attached to a grudging attitude. Annoyance, Pain and affliction, a sense of frustration, to be offended.

This word occurs in:

a) <u>John 16:6</u> and is translated "sorrow". Because of Jesus' prophecy regarding His death, sorrow filled the disciples' hearts.

b) <u>John 16:21</u> and is translated "sorrow". Jesus used this word to describe the pain of labor, and the contrast of the joy of the birth of a child.

c) II <u>Corinthians 2: 1-3</u> and is translated "heaviness" Paul determined not to come to the church at Corinth with annoyance and frustration because of their attitudes.

d) <u>II Corinthians 2:1</u> and is translated "sorrow". The verse reads "So that contrariwise ye ought rather to forgive him and comfort him, lest perhaps such a one should be swallowed up with overmuch sorrow". This verse denotes that another force is at work outside of the person's human soul. There an overwhelming sense of something which seeks to devour and destroy. (John 10:10)

e) <u>II Corinthians 7:10</u> and is translated "sorrow". This indicates there is a choice to be made as to whether the person involved will run into the arms of Jesus, and be hidden in Him, or if he will give in to the forces around him and be overpowered and pushed down.

ta'aniyah (tah-an-ee-yaw)	It means to mourn or grieve
This word occurs in:	a) <u>Isaiah 29:2</u> and is translated "heaviness". This verse is written to a rebellious Jerusalem, who has turned from a loving and generous God. *(Ariel is a symbolic name for Jerusalem --Nave's Topical).* At this point of the process, the person's will begins to turn toward rebelling against Father God, and the wall building begins within the soul. The rebellion of self-reliance and self- trust begin to take hold, and a hardness begins to cover the grief.

Antidote for this layer: At this point the person has begun to believe the lies of the adversary, and usually has become bitter at God, or if not at God, most generally at those around them. They isolate themselves and hide behind walls of indifference, work, or fear. Within this layer of depression, rebellion has begun its evil work, and it must be repented of.

(Note: To repent means more than just to be sorry and acknowledge the wrong. To repent means to turn away from the behavior pattern and seek the Lord with all of your heart, seeking not to give place to the sin ever again). Many times a person with this deep of a depression has one single bruise, which seeks to keep them in bondage to the depression --a molestation, a hurt, a tie of some kind to the past. There must be a cutting off (by the person's own confession) of any tie to the past. All three of the previous antidotes must be applied daily for this person to walk free. Isaiah 61: 3 says that the Lord gives "the oil of joy for mourning", although it is not the same Hebrew word as used here. The anointing with oil (a type of the Holy Spirit) to "break the yoke of bondage" is helpful, with a specific indication as an anointing with "the oil of joy or gladness".

Layer Five

#85(Greek) ademoneo   (ad-ay-mon-eh-o)   It means to be very heavy, to be full of heaviness to be troubled and in great distress or anguish. Depressed.

This word occurs in: a) <u>Matthew 26:37</u> and is translated "heavy". Jesus experienced this depression for us in the Garden of Gethsemane. He resisted it to the point of shedding blood. (Luke 22:44 describes the intense battle in the garden. The English word agony translates "agonia" from the Greek, which means "a struggle for victory, a wrestling of severe mental struggles and emotions, anguish". In Hebrews 12:4, the writer admonishes the reader to resist sin, striving against it even unto blood. This does not mean that being depressed is a sin. It is comforting to realize that Jesus experienced depression.)

b) <u>Mark 14:33</u> and is translated "heavy". This is the same account as Matthew 26:37, with the usage of the same Greek word.

#5136 (Hebrew)   nuwsh (noosh)   It means to be physically sick

This word occurs in: a) <u>Psalm 69:20</u> (only occurrence of this word in the entire Hebrew text). It is translated "heaviness". The verse reads "Reproach has broken by heart and I am full of heaviness" --(sick at heart, and possibly in body). This indicates that the end result of depression is a sickness.

Thought:
Is it possible that the completed end result of depression is mental illness?

<u>Antidote for this Layer:</u> *Jesus suffered for our emotional healing in the Garden of Gethsemane. His blood was shed there in the resistance against sin, during a violent wrestling. The only antidote for this depth of depression is the blood of Jesus. Daily cleansing through communion and confession with a trustworthy prayer-partner-minister, over each "brick in the wall" the person has built with depression will bring freedom and peace. Also, each of the other antidotes should be applied to the soul daily and as needed. Trusting in the wrong things to bring healing needs to be repented of as well.*

Proverbs 12:25	Heaviness in the heart of man causes depression, but a good word makes it glad. (Webster)
Psalm 61:3	To appoint unto them that mourn in Zion, to give unto them beauty For ashes, the oil of joy for mourning, the garment of praise for the spirit of heaviness; that they might be called trees of righteousness, the planting of the LORD, that he might be glorified. (KJV)
Psalm 69:20	Reproach hath broken my heart; and I am full of heaviness: and I looked [for some] to take pity, but [there was] none; and for comforters, but I found none. (KJV)
Proverbs 13:12	Hope deferred makes the heart sick: but [when] the desire cometh, [it is] a tree of life. (KJV)
John 14:16-18	And I will pray the Father, and he shall give you another Comforter, that he may abide with you forever; Even the Spirit of truth; whom the world cannot receive, because it does not see him, neither knows him: but ye know him; for he dwells with you, and shall be in you. I will not leave you comfortless: I will come to you.

Note: There is always a link between fear and depression. For a more thorough understanding of the fear issues involved in a client's depression, and how to help them, please refer to "A Christian Counselor's Primer on Fear and Anxiety (Book 2)" by Debbye Graafsma, also part of this series.

Many times, depression is part of the human condition, because of attachment needs within a person's soul. In my own experience in counseling, I have discovered a connection between unmet bonding needs in childhood and a person's inability to relate well to the people they are in relationship with in adulthood. On the next page, is a chart of attachment needs as they relate to the IQ and EQ levels of relationship/Communication. In the right column, I have listed Scriptures which correspond to the attachment core need in question. In providing this chart, it was to help clients to understand how Father God desires to connect and relate to each of us; especially in regard to the Core Desire listed.

Human Core Desires

For Healthy Relationships

1. To be noticed — I Samuel 16:7
2. To be complimented — Ephesians 4:32

3. To be seen — Genesis 16:6-13
4. To be included — Ephesians 2:1-10
5. To be safe (physically) — Psalm 62:8
6. To be affirmed — Psalm 116:1-9

~~~~~~

7. To experience safe touch — Luke 4:18/ Ps. 147:3
8. To be heard (to connect) — Isaiah 1:18
9. To belong (in a group) — Psalm 116:1-9
10. To be received — Psalm 34:15

11. To be trusted (emotionally safe) — James 2:23/Ex 33:11
12. To be chosen — Jeremiah 31:3
13. To be understood (to reciprocate connect) — Psalm 139
14. To be wanted — Ephesians 1:6

~~~~~~

15. To be secure — Psalm 103:8-12/Ps. 18:6-19
16. To be preferred — John 15:15
17. To be passionately desired — Ephesians 1:3-5

©2010 dg/atg

Lies That Tie Us to Oppression/Heaviness

The Lie: "God expects me to do things perfectly."
 The Truth: Galatians 3:3
  II Cor. 12:9
  Psalm 18:32

The Lie: "I need to keep a perfect environment."

 The Truth: II Samuel 22:33

The Lie: "I must please everyone; I must keep everyone happy."

 The Truth: Colossians 2:6-8

The Lie: "I need everyone's approval."

 The Truth: Galatians 1:10

The Lie: "I need to be like everyone else in order to be right."

 The Truth: II Corinthians 10:12

The Lie: "I must defend myself, or no one will.."

 The Truth: Psalm 31:15
  Psalm 91:1-3
  Psalm 119:114

The Lie: "I must create a place for myself."

 The Truth: Proverbs 18:16

The Lie: "Close relationships with other people are dangerous."

 The Truth: Eccl. 4:9-12
  Proverbs 27:9-10;
  Proverbs 18:24

The Lie: "Being vulnerable is unsafe. I can't tell anyone my struggles."

 The Truth: James 5:16
  Eph. 4:13-15

The Lie: "I am on the outside. I don't belong."

 The Truth: Ephesians 1:3-12

The Lie: "I must earn my place."

 The Truth: II Timothy 1:9
  Titus 3:5-7

The Lie: "What I do determines my worth."

 The Truth: Matt. 10:26-31
  Luke 12:6-7
  Ephesians 2:8-10
  Psalm 139:14-18

The Lie: "God does not want to talk to me."

 The Truth: John 16:12-15

The Lie: "I must take the blame for there to be peace in my relationships."

 The Truth: Galatians 6:5

The Lie: "Love and sexual expression are the same thing.."

 The Truth: I Thess. 4:3-8
  I Corinthians 13

The Lie: "Conflict is always bad."

 The Truth: Ephesians 6:12

The Lie: "I can't trust anyone else with my heart, and my inner desires."

 The Truth: Ephesians 5:21
  I Cor. 13:4-7

The Lie: "I must make my own way."

 The Truth: I Peter 3:8-9

The Lie: "Respect and fear are the same thing. I must fear authority."

 The Truth: II Timothy 1:7
  Romans 8:15-17

The Lie: "I must protect my own interests to be heard, and to be safe."
  The Truth: Philippians 2:3-4
  I Peter 4:8-11

The Lie: "I must be in control to be heard and to be safe."

  The Truth: Deut. 30:6

The Lie: "When things go wrong, God doesn't accept me. There is something wrong with me."
  The Truth: Ephesians 2:4-7
  Hebrews 4:14-16

The Lie: "It is too late for me to change. Too much has happened."

  The Truth: Hebrews 12:1-2

The Lie: "Anger is my empowerment to speak and be heard."

  The Truth: Eph. 4:26-27
  James 1:19

The Lie: "Alcohol will make me feel better."

  The Truth: Proverbs 23:29-32

The Lie: "Pain is part of intimacy. Intimacy must be avoided for me to be safe."

  The Truth: John 15:4-8
  Heb. 10:24-25

The Lie: "God likes other people more than He likes me."

  The Truth: Romans 2:11

The Lie: "I must make my own way.."

  The Truth: Psalm 138:7-8

The Lie: "My feelings determine truth for me."
  The Truth: Philippians 4:8

The Lie: "My perceptions and experiences determine truth."

  The Truth: Phil. 1:9-11
  Psalm 51:6

The Lie: "When people don't agree with me, they don't love me."

  The Truth: Proverbs 11:3
  Proverbs 17:9
  Proverbs 27:6

The Lie: "God is mean, and I must earn His love."
  The Truth: Psalm 103:8-14

The Lie: "The bad things that happen in my life are in indication of God's will for me."

  The Truth: Jer. 29:11-13
  II Samuel 22:3

The Lie: "I need to protect my own interests."

  The Truth: Psalm 5:11

The Lie: "When things are not going well for me, I do not have God's acceptance and approval."

  The Truth: James 1:2-4

The Lie: "God likes other people more than He likes me. He must have favorites."
  The Truth: Romans 2:11

The Lie: "It's too late for me to change."
  The Truth: Hebrews 12:1-2

The Lie: "Life can't be any better than this. I'm stuck."
  The Truth: Romans 8:28
  Jer. 29:11-13

Section Seven
Scriptural Prayer and Supportive Materials

To Overcome Depression

*"For I will turn their mourning into joy, and will comfort them,
and make them rejoice from their sorrow. "*
Jeremiah 31:13

The book of Proverbs says: "Hope deferred makes the heart sick." (Proverbs 13:12) When a person is depressed, it is an indication of a legitimate need or desire in the life, which has remained unfulfilled. If adult depression cannot be linked to a particular instance, such as a loss or a death, it is tied to childhood trauma, and the person's inability to combine present life experience with past life memories. The answer is to find contentment in the Presence of Father God, choosing to put into His hands the situation and its solution. He holds the answer. Depression occurs because the human emotions and mental capacity can find no real solution on its own. Contentment is found through giving praise (Isaiah 61:3 -"the mantle of praise instead of a spirit of fainting"), and through focusing upon the Father rather than one's own needs and desires. Many times, choosing to become a servant within a local fellowship can help to begin the process of freedom from depression. This does not suggest that a person should not confront the depression, however. Service should never be used as an escape from inner battle.

The difficulty in dealing with natural depression is finding the balance between comfort and confrontation. A depressed person must be comforted where there is legitimate difficulty, but they must also be confronted in areas where they have allowed themselves to become inwardly focused. When confrontation makes no recognizable difference, the problem can usually be linked to demonic attack and oppression. These forces must be aggressively confronted with the Word of God, the Blood of the Lamb, and prayer, in every area where they have caused a shell to develop over the human soul.

It will help to pray in this manner:

Father God, I confess my discouragement and depression to you. It is my choice to repent for allowing my inner focus to become centered upon myself, and my own heart, rather than upon You and Your love for me. I choose to let go of my selfishness and my right to be depressed. I choose to seek Your Will and Way for my life. I open the door of my soul to your love for me. Please wash away everything that stands in the way of my receiving your perfect and unconditional love.

Lord, I confess that Your Word says that you are close to those who are of a broken heart, and that you save those who have a contrite (apologetic and remorseful) spirit. You heal the broken heart and bind up those wounds. You have promised to give beauty in the place of ashes, gladness for mourning, and to restore comforts to those in need of healing. You have promised to turn my mourning into joy and to deliver me out of all of my afflictions. You have said that if I will cast my burdens upon You, that you will sustain me. It is my choice to give you all of my burdens. They are too heavy for me.

Lord, Your Word says that your eyes are upon me, and your ears are open to my cry. You desire to give me peace, and to comfort me, making me to rejoice from my sorrow. Even though I am in the midst of a dark night now, you have promised to bring me joy in the morning. I choose to believe that it is your desire to give me beauty for ashes, joy for mourning, and a heart filled with praise instead of this heaviness. I open my heart and choose to wait upon you to renew my strength.

Your joy is my strength. You will help me. It is my will not to give up and not to be weary.

You have promised to uphold me with your right hand, and to be always be with me. You have promised that sorrow and mourning will flee away from me, and that I will obtain gladness and joy.

Depression, the Blood of the Lamb is against you. You have no authority to speak to me, because I choose to remove every legal right I have given you to deal in my life. I choose not to listen to you, but to listen to what the Word of God says about my life. Depression, you cannot speak into my life, or influence me, because my hope is in the Lord Jesus Christ and His work upon the Cross for me. I do not even have to fight this battle, for the battle is not mine, but it belongs to the Lord. You have been defeated by the death of the Son of God, and I will not give you place any longer.

Psalm 34:15,17	Isaiah 61:3	Psalm 34:18-19	Psalm 55:22	Isaiah 57:19
II Thess. 2:16-17	Jer. 31:13b	Isaiah 43:2	Psalm 30:5	Isaiah 66:13a
Isaiah 40:31	II Cor. 1:3-4	Romans 8:38-39	Psalm 147:3	Isaiah 41:10
I Peter 5:6-7	Neh. 8:10	Isaiah 51:11		

Scriptural Answers to Depression and Futility

When Depression and Futility say	"I'm too tired."	
The Spirit of the Living God replies	"I will give you rest."	(Matthew 11:28-30)
When Depression and Futility say	"I can't go on."	
The Spirit of the Living God replies	"My grace is sufficient for you."	(II Cor. 12:9) (Psalm 91:5)
When Depression and Futility say	"I am all alone."	
The Spirit of the Living God replies	"I am always with you."	(Hebrews 13:5)
When Depression and Futility say	"It just can't happen."	
The Spirit of the Living God replies	"With Me all things are possible."	(Luke 18:27)
When Depression and Futility say	"I don't know how."	
The Spirit of the Living God replies	"I am able."	(II Corinthians 9:8)
When Depression and Futility say	"I'm not lovable."	
The Spirit of the Living God replies	"I love you more than you know."	(John 3:34)
When Depression and Futility say	"I don't know where to go."	
The Spirit of the Living God replies	"I will guide you."	(Proverbs 3:5-6)
When Depression and Futility say	"It's not worth it."	
The Spirit of the Living God replies	"There is only good ahead."	(Romans 8:28) (Jeremiah 29:11)
When Depression and Futility say	"I've done too much to forgive."	(Romans 8:1-2)
The Spirit of the Living God replies	"But I will forgive you."	(I John 1:9)
When Depression and Futility say	"Be afraid."	
The Spirit of the Living God replies	"I will give you power and a sound mind."	(II Tim 1:7)
When Depression and Futility say	"I'm not smart enough."	
The Spirit of the Living God replies	"I will give wisdom."	(I Corinthians 1:30)
When Depression and Futility say	"I can't."	
The Spirit of the Living God replies	"I will give you the strength to finish."	(Philippians 4:13)
When Depression and Futility say	"I don't have enough."	
The Spirit of the Living God replies	"I will supply what you need."	(Philippians 4:19)

Suggested Reading List – Depression

Breaking Through Depression: A Biblical and Medical Approach to Emotional Wholeness by Donald P. Hall

A Christian's Guide to Depression and Antidepressants by Gregory Knopf, Alane Pearce and Nathan Fisher

Overcoming Anxiety and Depression: Practical Tools to Help you Deal with Negative Emotions by Bob Phillips

Overcoming Depression: The Victory Over the Darkness Series by Neil T. Anderson and Joanne Anderson

The Masks of Melancholy: A Christian Physician looks at Depression and Suicide by John White, MD

www.ingramcontent.com/pod-product-compliance
Lightning Source LLC
Chambersburg PA
CBHW080347170426
43194CB00014B/2716